CAESAR'S GREAT SUCCESS

CAESAR'S GREAT SUCCESS

SUSTAINING THE ROMAN ARMY ON CAMPAIGN

Alexander Merrow, Agostino von Hassell
and Gregory Starace

Dear Mr. Hoffman,
Thank you for encouraging me
to have a love for military history
from when I was young. I hope you
enjoy reading this as much as I did
writing it.

DOCENDO
DISCIMUS,

Gregory Starace

FRONTLINE
BOOKS

MIX
Paper from
responsible sources
FSC® C013056
www.fsc.org

Published in 2020 by Frontline Books,
an imprint of Pen & Sword Books Ltd,
47 Church Street, Barnsley, S. Yorkshire, S70 2AS

www.frontline-books.com

ISBN: 978 1 47385 587 8

For more information on our books, please visit www.frontline-books.com, email
info@frontline-books.com or write to us at the above address.

Printed and bound by
TJ International Ltd, Padstow, Cornwall
Typeset by Donald Sommerville

Pen & Sword Books Ltd incorporates the imprints of Pen & Sword Archaeology,
Atlas, Aviation, Battleground, Discovery, Family History, History, Maritime,
Military, Naval, Politics, Social History, Transport, True Crime, Claymore Press,
Frontline Books, Praetorian Press, Seaforth Publishing and White Owl

For a complete list of Pen and Sword titles please contact

PEN & SWORD LTD
47 Church Street, Barnsley, South Yorkshire, S70 2AS, England
E-mail: enquiries@pen-and-sword.co.uk
Or
PEN AND SWORD BOOKS
1950 Lawrence Rd, Havertown, PA 19083, USA
E-mail: Uspen-and-sword@casematepublishers.com

Contents

List of Plates
Images courtesy of Agostino von Hassell

Chronology

vii

56 BC   Campaigns against the Veneti. In Rome, the triumvirate of Caesar, Pompey and Crassus renewed.

55 BC   The Germanic Usipetes and Tencteri tribes crossed the Rhine and invaded Gaul. Roman forces stopped them and pursued them back over the Rhine into Germania in a punitive expedition. Later, Caesar crossed the Channel to Britannia with two legions.

54 BC   Caesar returned to Britannia with five legions and defeated the Catuvellauni.

53 BC   Caesar crossed the Rhine a second time. Ambiorix, leader of a Belgic tribe, raised an uprising of Gallic forces against the Romans. Elsewhere, Crassus is killed fighting the Parthians at Carrhae. Pompey soon becomes sole consul in Rome, leading to tensions between Pompey and Caesar.

52 BC   General Gallic uprising under Vercingetorix, chief of the Arverni tribe, culminating in the Battle of Alesia.

51 BC   Roman control of Gaul was secure.

49 BC   Caesar crossed the Rubicon, initiating the Civil War. Pompey and consuls left Rome. Caesar called the Senate in Rome. Caesar defeated Afranius and Petrius near Ilerda and Caesarean forces began siege of Massilia. Defeat of Antonius in Illyria. Caesar began first dictatorship in Rome.

48 BC   Caesar made consul with P. Servilius. Caesar crossed the Adriatic to Illyria. Caesar defeated at Dyrrachium. Caesar defeated Pompey at the Battle of Pharsalus. Pompey killed in Egypt after fleeing Pharsalus. Caesar arrived in Alexandria, Egypt.

47 BC   Caesar's dictatorship renewed for one year. Caesar defeated rebellious forces of Cleopatra's brother. Caesar defeated Pharnaces at Zela in Pontus. Caesar crossed to North Africa.

46 BC   Caesar made consul for third time and dictator for another 10 years. Caesar defeated Pompey loyalists at Thaspus. Caesar returned to Rome. Caesar left Rome for Spain.

45 BC   Caesar made consul for fourth time and dictator for life. Pompey's sons defeated at Munda. Caesar returned to Rome and celebrated triumph in Spain.

44 BC   Caesar made consul for fifth time. Caesar is murdered.

Introduction

A great strategy is to press the enemy more
with famine than with the sword.

Vegetius, *Epitome of Military Science*

What did logistics comprise in an age without munitions or fuel and soldiers who carried almost everything they needed to fight? Interestingly, the Romans did not have a word that directly translates to 'logistics'. The term that comes closest, *res frumentaria*, appears only rarely in Caesar's works.[1] Logistics was about food. Gaius Julius Caesar's logistical wizardry meant he was, in many ways, a culinary genius. His influence on military manoeuvres such as food transportation and supply, as well as cooking in the field and at the commissary, has been pervasive. Techniques devised by Caesar for moving a well-nourished army into hostile territory while retaining the ability to supply its need for nutritional food while on campaign, though developed and first implemented over 2,000 years ago, are still in evidence in modern military campaigns. In fact, one could argue that Julius Caesar's great success was feeding his army while on campaign. Caesar has never received the recognition he deserves for being as ingenious and inventive when it came to the care and feeding of a mobile army as he was at logistics.

We have come to know mobility and the movement of supplies in their contemporary, facile and efficient forms. Today, sufficient bottled water is stored in global hot spots before it is needed and water purification devices are readily available. MREs – meals ready to eat, military precooked ration packs – ensure soldiers have sufficient calories and nutrients, even in the direst circumstances. Computers tabulate and are programmed to order the restocking of low supplies, whether food, fuel or ammunition. Commanders evaluate supply levels and transportation routes on large-screen high-definition monitors, analyzing connections between any point on the globe and any other point on the globe, at any hour of the day or night. Yet Caesar had none of this and still he pioneered and accomplished so much. In his time, movement and communication were limited to transportation by manpower, wind power, horsepower, camel or even elephant power.

In Caesar's time people's horizons, as well as their news networks, were typically limited to their particular settlement, village or town and to their extended family, clan or tribe. News travelled slowly and was rarely disseminated widely. Most of it was transmitted by word of mouth. Occasionally there would be contact with non-kin neighbouring peoples through raids or warfare or possibly through trade. People could live in one settlement, village or town all their lives, never travelling farther from its centre than perhaps 25 miles (40km) or so. This generally limited the world perspective to what was physically experienced and what was passed by word of mouth from those who had ventured beyond the familiar. Except for migratory peoples travelling remarkable distances along their timeless routes, most people were what we today would consider virtual hermits.

With all these limitations staring him in the face, Caesar was nevertheless able to move his legions through Gaul, Britannia and Germania, covering vast distances extending into unknown and unmapped territories. He managed, against great odds, not only to protect his troops but to house, fortify and feed them well. To say he was inventive and resourceful in accomplishing this unprecedented feat is an understatement. It was astonishing, pulled off without what we today call geospatial intelligence. Verbal reports brought back by exploratory parties who made limited sorties into these unknown lands or through scouts recruited from indigenous populations were all that was available. These lands were fraught with natural dangers and populated by primitive and hostile clans and tribes – sometimes even whole armies. For briefings, Caesar had only bare-bones verbal reports without detailed maps or overhead imagery to use to lay out operational strategies and itineraries or detail applicable logistics to facilitate them.

The maps at Caesar's disposal showed no details of terrain he would encounter nor the forms of hostile resistance he might face. No bird's-eye views, aerial photography or satellite images, no system to collect and process personal accounts from boots-on-the-ground scouts. Given these conditions, how did Caesar execute the campaigns of exploration and conquest confident that his army would be properly nourished? How did he supplement the grain ration with sufficiently nutritious foods?

While planning these logistics, Caesar used the roads and cartography the Romans had developed in their homeland and in places they had already conquered. These gave him the comparative engineering advantage he needed in operational planning. It allowed him to move men, animals and wagons from one end of the Republic or the Empire to another in the fastest and most efficient manner possible in antiquity.

Julius Caesar, of course, considered the landscape in the conduct of his wars. In other words, geography and climate played a role and different factors were prominent in Gaul, in Spain, the Balkans and North Africa, each with the region's own ecological restraints regarding agriculture, transportation and the economies and peoples of the region. Ecology played a particularly significant role, proven by the fact that Caesar's campaigns generally ceased as winter approached and his legions retreated to winter quarters. Only when conditions improved – conditions that allowed the sustenance of a large, mobile army – did they return to the campaign against their enemies.

Enabled by road networks and the catalogue of maps, Caesar devised the multi-faceted and multi-layered system that supplied Rome's legions with items and foodstuffs from across the Mediterranean. Some of these supplies were provided within a particular province, others were transported vast distances from their point of origin and still others were brought with the legion and then replicated locally at the bivouac, encampment or fortress where the campaign had taken them. Most important, if the enemy had pursued a scorched-earth policy while retreating before Caesar's legions, this sophisticated Roman supply system allowed Caesar to continue feeding his troops despite the enemy having eliminated the possibility of foraging.

Herein lies the crux of Caesar's logistical genius. We will show exactly what was entailed in feeding a legion and how Caesar fed 5,000 men while on campaign, in garrison, or in the field. Consider how legionaries relied heavily on forage, when and where possible, to augment a supply chain that provided staples and essentials. Caesar and his legionaries took advantage of tried and trusted food items that were durable, nutritious and readily available. All of these logistical practices were crucial to Caesar's success; he often campaigned with several 5,000-man legions, all of whom needed to be fed. An old military truism, often attributed to Napoleon, says, 'an army marches on its stomach', and an underfed and undernourished army is always an ineffective army – and often a defeated one. That fate rarely befell Caesar's legions.

Caesar's own accounts of the Gallic and Civil Wars are our best source regarding the Roman military food supply during those campaigns. He paid such attention to food supply for two reasons. First, food supply clearly played a central role in his campaigns. It often determined when and where battles and entire campaigns took place.

Second, Caesar prided himself on his ability to feed his army. Along with speed and staying on the offensive, preparation was part of his presentation of himself as a successful general.[2] It is difficult to find in Caesar's writings a campaign that does not address the food supply, either of his army or that of his enemy.

Yet because Caesar's own works are our primary source, they must be read with a grain of caution. References to food supply are self-serving and lead to Caesar's portrayal as a logistical genius. It is quite probable that Caesar's troops were hungrier far more often than he allows. And when hunger is mentioned, it is often done for dramatic effect, to highlight the bravery and commitment of his men.

At the beginning of the campaigns in Gaul, the Roman troops had been supplied from Gallia Narbonensis, a Roman province located in what is now Languedoc and Provence. Grain was delivered along the Rhône while the Romans followed the Helvetii along the Saône.[3] This is the only provable case in the Gallic War in which the grain for the entire Roman army in Gaul was procured in Roman territory and delivered to the troops. Caesar was then forced to separate from the supply lines as the Helvetii moved farther away from the Saône. Along the roads and paths, Caesar could not provide for the 31 tons of grain needed for his six legions.[4] In other words, the Roman supply lines were insufficient and as soon as the transport needed to move over land, there were severe limitations. The lines were so incapable that Caesar – because foraging and the purchase of grain was not possible at the time and using the Aedui to supply the Romans was no longer possible – abandoned his original campaign plan. He gave up on following the Helvetii and had to march with his entire army to the capital of the Aedui.[5]

Crucial to this system was the Roman military's marching camp. A forerunner of the modern military's 'firm base', the marching camp provided an island of protection for troops and supplies as they advanced into hostile territory. Caesar understood the marching camp's unique ability to enhance the endurance of his legions, greatly expanding the safety and range of operations. Moreover, by expanding his army's range and reach, the marching camp encouraged Caesar's contact with a variety of fruits, vegetables, grains and game and brought Caesar and his legions into contact with different styles of cuisine.

The most astute and perceptive operational planners recognized the necessity of an excellent quartermaster corps. Caesar's savvy, supported by a superb quartermaster corps, allowed him to wage campaign after campaign, each time planning for the distances to be travelled and the commissary challenges to be met. When his troops arrived at the scene of battle, they were well fed and in full fighting trim. Thus Caesar leveraged the full force of his legions against his enemies.

The questions that shape this book – how did commanders feed an army so far from home, what did the soldiers eat and drink, how much did the individual soldier carry, what role did requisitioning and the local economy play, how were food supply and strategy linked – could be asked of wars throughout history, yet Caesar's accomplishment was not replicated until two millennia later. His great success begs a closer look. Beginning with a thematic overview of Caesar's biography, the Gallic and Civil Wars and a calculation of the size of the Caesarean army, the book then looks into the food for battle, what the Roman soldiers ate and drank while on campaign, with attention given to calorific and nutritional needs and a brief look at eating habits. The basics of logistics – administration, infrastructure, personnel – are important in order to understand how foodstuffs were brought from sources of supply along sea, river and land routes to the soldiers on the march, where their supplies were complemented with forage and regulated plunder. Requisition of grain from allies and defeated foes was an enormous source of supply. Additional topics are relevant, from how individuals carried food and cooking utensils to the relationship between logistics and strategy. Logistics differed from the Gallic War to the Civil War and thus so did strategy. Finally, we provide Caesar's accomplishment with a modern comparison, in which remarkable similarities in logistics and strategy become obvious. Caesar left a legacy, though not only in logistics. Caesar's campaigns also had tremendous impacts on the development of food history, first in Europe and eventually throughout the world.

Former United States Marine Corps Commandant Alfred M. Gray, Jr. stated, 'As we select our forces and plan our operations, we must understand how logistics can impact on our concepts of operation . . . Commanders must base all their concepts of operation on what they know they can do logistically.' For brilliantly executing logistics more than 2,000 years ago and for leaving a legacy in this crucial aspect of military campaigning that endures to this day, Caesar deserves abundant credit.

This book is about food and cuisine as much as it is about logistics. In Caesar's time, these were largely the same. Caesar sampled and incorporated new foods into his own diet and that of his troops, along with the manner in which the indigenous people prepared, cooked and served them. Upon his return to Rome, Caesar introduced these ingredients and their styles of preparation to the capital of the known world and they spread the length and breadth of the empire. Their legacy is in European cuisine worldwide today.

The topic allows for a little fun – and an opportunity to share some recipes from the Ancient World, recipes that are one of the greatest legacies of Caesar's influence on the world. Modern European cuisine was heavily impacted by Caesar's campaigns and this cuisine has been translated today to both American continents as well as to Asia, Africa and Oceania. It now covers the globe and in turn has been influenced by every local cuisine it has come into contact with. The culinary prowess of such cross-pollination has been facilitated more by the military than by any other means, including diplomatic or expeditionary. Everyone knows how Marco Polo brought Chinese noodles back to Venice and kick-started the Italian legerdemain with pasta, starting with the simple but superb dish known as spaghetti. Yet how many people know whether it's true that Caesar is responsible for yet another classic of European cuisine known as coq au vin, the glorious chicken in wine sauce dish found even in the most humble of backstreet brasseries in Paris? And what about the derivation of a Caesar salad? What does it have to do with its namesake? On such matters we intend to shed some light.

Caesar's influence on aspects of modern European cuisine is considerable, yet it has been studied, written up and even extolled in a way that slighted its deep military provenance. We intend to give a flavour of the foods eaten, both by the soldiers and by the officers

Oysters with Sauce

Sergius Orata of the Roman Republic is credited with being the first large-scale commercial cultivator of the molluscs. Oysters were regarded as a subsistence food by Britons until the Romans arrived and created demand for all types of seafood. In the United Kingdom, oyster beds on the Kentish Flats have been providing food since the Roman times. Their quality was renowned and they were shipped all the way to Rome. Apicius provided a savoury recipe for oysters with cumin sauce. This modern adaptation includes cumin, but stimulates more of the taste buds, combining sweet, sour and savoury flavours.

Ingredients:

2 dozen oysters, washed and scrubbed clean and chilled
1 Tbsp olive oil
3–4 scallions, chopped
1–2 Tbsp lovage leaves, finely chopped
½ tsp caraway seed, crushed
¾ tsp cumin seed, crushed
1 Tbsp honey
3 Tbsp red wine vinegar
50ml/2 fl oz Dijon (or grainy style) mustard
Cracked black pepper to taste
Snipped chive to taste

Directions:

In a small saucepan, heat oil and add scallions and lovage. Sauté for one minute until softened. Add caraway, cumin and honey and bring to a boil. Add vinegar and mustard and stir until incorporated. Remove from heat.

Preheat oven to 190°C/375°F/Gas 5.

Shuck the oysters, discarding the top flat shell and place on a baking sheet. (Hint: pour some coarse salt on the tray to keep the oysters from tipping and spilling their liquid.) Place a teaspoon of sauce on each oyster. Bake in the preheated oven for 8 to 10 minutes. Remove and garnish with cracked black pepper and snipped chive.

Serves 4

Chapter 1

Julius Caesar, His Wars and The Caesarean Army

An army marches on its stomach.

Napoleon

Julius Caesar's Gallic and Civil Wars are familiar terrain. Nonetheless, because this book is thematic – detailing how Julius Caesar fed his army while on campaign – a brief overview of Caesar's wars provides necessary narrative structure, which will help the reader put the anecdotes and references into context. Furthermore, in order to appreciate how significant Caesar's logistical accomplishments were, it is important to grasp the size of his army and to calculate just how many mouths – and maws – he had to feed. This chapter aims to provide a brief overview of Caesar's wars and to compute the size of Caesar's army.

Caesar's Career Prior to the Gallic Wars

Julius Caesar's family rose to prominence in the generation before Caesar's birth. The patrician family, which claimed descent from the goddess Venus, was of Alban origin and had settled in Rome, though there is little evidence of political influence until Caesar's father, also called Gaius Julius Caesar, became consul in the Roman province of Asia (today western Turkey) and Caesar's aunt married Gaius Marius, a prominent Roman general and statesman. Caesar's mother, Aurelia Cotta, also came from a wealthy and influential family.

The sudden death of his father in 85 BC elevated Caesar to head of the family at the age of 16. At the time, a civil war raged between Lucius Cornelius Sulla, a general and statesman whom many see as having set a precedent for Caesar's later march on Rome and dictatorship, and Caesar's uncle, Gaius Marius. While Marius and his ally Lucius Cornelius Cinna controlled the city, Caesar ascended to the position of *Flamen Dialis*, the high priest of Jupiter, and married Cinna's daughter Cornelia. Sulla eventually emerged victorious, however, and Caesar was stripped of his priesthood as well as his own inheritance and Cornelia's dowry. Caesar feared Sulla's further wrath and joined the army in order to get away from the dictator. The contrast between his old position and his new could not be greater, as the *Flamen Dialis* was forbidden to sit on a horse, be in the presence of an army or sleep for a single night outside of Rome. Quite simply, stripping Caesar of his priestly title allowed a path to the Gallic Wars. During his early military career, Caesar served under Marcus Minucius Thermus in Asia and Servilius Isauricus in Cicilia. He fought in the Siege of Mytilene in 81 BC, winning a Civic Crown, the second highest decoration to which a citizen could aspire.

Upon Sulla's death in 78 BC, Caesar returned to Rome. Although without means, he gained attention as a legal advocate and was known for his prosecution of corruption and extortion. His oratorical skills, complete with dramatic gestures and a high-pitched voice, won him praise and support in many parts of the city.

Several events and anecdotes from this period in Caesar's life shed light on his actions and motivations during the Gallic and Civil Wars. Pirates kidnapped Caesar while he was crossing the Aegean Sea and he was insulted when they demanded a ransom twenty talents of silver. He insisted they ask for fifty. He also promised to capture and crucify his captors. When the ransom was paid, he raised a fleet and did just that. The punishment was swift and carried out on his own authority. Later, in 69 BC, while serving his quaestorship in Spain, Caesar came across a statue of Alexander the Great. He is said to have realized that by the time Alexander was his age, he had conquered the world. Caesar, in contrast, had accomplished little. This suggests that Caesar considered himself capable of comparable feats.

Caesar returned to Rome in 67 BC and married Sulla's granddaughter, Pompeia, suggesting a desire to bring warring factions together. Two years later, Caesar was elected *aedile*, the office responsible for maintaining public buildings and organizing festivals. The popular games he staged drew considerable attention and public support for his abilities.

In the next years, Caesar served in numerous positions, including *Pontifex Maximus* (63 BC), the most senior position in the Roman religion, *praetor* (62 BC) and subsequently *propraetor* of Hispania Ulterior. The latter position drew him closer to Marcus Licinius

Crassus, who paid off Caesar's debts in exchange for political support. Caesar's governorship in Spain was praised, having reformed laws and conducting two victorious military campaigns against local tribes. His troops hailed him as *imperator*, but rather than applying for a triumph – the ceremony celebrating the commander who had led forces to victory – Caesar instead opted to stand for consul, the highest magistracy in the Republic. Caesar won the sordid election and served as consul in 59 BC.

Already politically close to Crassus, Caesar made overtures to Pompey, Crassus' long-time political enemy. Together the three men formed an informal alliance – the First Triumvirate – and were able to sideline the other consul elected for the year, Marcus Bibulus, and exert tremendous political influence. Moreover, Pompey married Caesar's daughter, Julia, cementing the relationship.

In the later Roman Republic, consuls were often given a governorship of a province outside of Rome and the title of proconsul. Proconsuls were given full consular powers and included the command of an army. Yet the aristocracy feared Caesar's future power and granted him the rather opaque and meaningless title of governor of the woods and pastures of Italy, a position that excluded military service and provided little opportunity for Caesar to overcome his persistent personal debts. Caesar enlisted the help of political allies and won an alternative governorship, that of Cisalpine Gaul (northern Italy) and Illyricum (south-eastern Europe). Transalpine Gaul (southern France) was later added. In all, Caesar had command of four legions. He quickly left for his province at the end of his consulship and began an unusually long five-year term.

Caesar's political career begs the question of what positions and roles helped him develop his logistical acumen. By the time he had taken command of an army, he had held virtually every important office in the Roman government. Certainly, as consul and to a lesser extent *praetor*, he dealt with the management of resources and supplies and this no doubt gave him valuable experience. However, no small part of his logistical education were episodes of poor logistical planning in the early stages of the Gallic War that taught him valuable lessons. These incidents include having to call off the pursuit of Dumnorix and the Helvetii in 58 BC and Ariovistus cutting off Roman supplies shortly thereafter. Indeed, there were countless moments during both the Gallic and the Civil War when the importance of supply was reinforced. So, while Caesar was not completely unprepared when he took command, much of his education was autodidactic.

A Brief History of Julius Caesar's Wars

Pompey and Crassus intervened and used popular assemblies to promote Caesar to Roman governor of Illyricum and Cisalpine Gaul. His term of office was an unusually long five years, a period in which he was immune from prosecution. The term was later extended another five years.

At the beginning of his governorship of these provinces, Caesar commanded four legions: Legio VII, Legio VIII, Legio IX Hispana and Legio X. Caesar knew these legions well, having campaigned with them against the Lusitanians while governor of Hispania Ulterior in 61 BC. He was fondest of Legio X, which Caesar had personally raised in Spain. The X played a prominent role in the Gallic campaigns and Caesar consistently extolled its virtues and bravery in his commentaries.

The beginning of the Gallic campaigns was not inconsistent with Roman security strategy. The Roman Republic sought stability on its northern border. Fifty years previously, the Republic had been invaded from the north, resulting in the Cimbrian War. Though Gaius Marius ultimately led Rome to victory in the conflict, the battles were costly and were seared into the Roman memory. Fear of new invasions was never far from military leaders' strategic thinking. Yet beyond the interest of stability to the north of the Republic, it cannot be denied that Caesar's persistent financial difficulties played a role in his subsequent involvement north of the Alps. The region was ripe for conquest and plunder and some tribes looked promising as potential allies. The Aedui, for example, traded regularly with the Romans and had joined previous political alliances. Caesar understood from the outset that sustaining military action in the region would require the assistance of allies.

A coalition of Arverni, Sequani and Suebi attacked the Aedui in 63 BC. After the Battle of Magetobria, the Aedui statesman and druid Diviciacus requested aid from Rome. The situation looked grim. Ariovistus, chief of the Suebi, demanded from his allies land in order to settle 120,000 of his people who themselves had been harassed by Germanic tribes to the east. The demand made Rome nervous. Ariovistus would soon be in a position to control all of the lands of the Sequani and could threaten attacks throughout Gaul. This could lead to mass migrations comparable to those of the Cimbrian War (113–101 BC), the only time since the Second Punic War that Italia had been seriously threatened.

When the Aedui were threatened again in 58 BC, Caesar, newly appointed governor of the Roman province of Transalpine Gaul, was not going to sit back and watch. This time it was the Helvetii, a confederation of five Gallic tribes, who were under pressure from the north and the east. The Helvetii planned a mass migration across Aedui lands and through Transalpine Gaul to the west coast of Gaul. They requested a grant of peaceful passage, yet showed little willingness to wait for Rome's response. The Helvetii leaders ordered the burning of their towns and villages, both to increase the commitment of the émigrés and to prevent enemies from taking the spoils of their abandoned lands.

Caesar was committed to stopping the passage of the Helvetii, but was in no position to respond. He was south of the Alps and there was but a single legion in Transalpine Gaul. He stalled negotiations, built defences, ordered the destruction of the Rhône bridge and immediately formed auxiliary units. Once better positioned, he rejected the Helvetii's plea for safe passage and warned that attempts to cross the Rhône would be met with force. Several attempts were made, but the Romans successfully repelled them, forcing the Helvetii to seek an alternate route.

Caesar rushed to Cisalpine Gaul, where he took command of three legions stationed in Aquileia. He also levied two new legions, Legio XI and Legio XII, and led the five legions through the Alps to stop the Helvetii on their new routes. The Helvetii, meanwhile, had crossed the territories of the Sequani and were plundering the lands of the Aedui, Allobroges and Ambarri, all Roman allies. Caesar accepted their request for aid and attacked the Helvetii as they crossed the Saône river. Caesar defeated the portion of the tribe that had not yet crossed the river and built a bridge over the Saône to pursue the remaining Helvetii.

It is noteworthy that Caesar's troops ran into early supply problems, due to treachery on the part of Dumnorix, an Aedui chieftain who thought it better to be dominated by fellow Gauls than by the Romans. Caesar pursued the Helvetii for two weeks but his army was in no position to fight effectively if they caught them. Instead, Caesar called off the pursuit and his troops retired to the Aedui town of Bibracte. The Helvetii turned and followed the Romans. The belligerents met and the Battle of Bibracte resulted in the sound defeat of the Helvetii. Caesar, recognizing the surviving Helvetii to be a useful buffer against the Germanic tribes to the north, ordered them to return to their homeland, a passage that received Roman assistance.

As a result of Caesar's defeat of the Helvetii, most Gallic tribes were eager to negotiate with him in order to enlist Rome's assistance in dealing with the threat of the Germanic invasion. In particular, they feared the recent Suebian land acquisition and were angered over the taking of hostages. The Gallic delegation appealed for Caesar to defeat Ariovistus, the king of the Suebi. Caesar acknowledged Rome's obligation to aid its allies, especially the Aedui. In addition, defeating the Suebi provided Caesar with opportunities: the Roman Republic would secure – and possibly expand – its northern borders and the Roman army's allegiance to Caesar as its leader would be strengthened.

Still, Caesar could not simply declare war on Ariovistus. The Roman Senate had recently declared him a 'king and friend of the Roman people'. But Caesar delivered an ultimatum to Ariovistus: the Aedui hostages were to be returned and no Germans were to cross the Rhine. Ariovistus countered that Rome should stay out of the internal affairs of those outside of the Republic's borders. The Harudes, an ally of the Suebi, attacked the Aedui in 58 BC and reports came in that large numbers of Suebi were trying to cross the Rhine into Gaul. Caesar had all the justification he needed and declared war on Ariovistus.

The Roman army – led by Caesar's beloved Legio X – marched to the well-fortified Sequani town of Vesontio (Besançon) upon word that Ariovistus intended to seize the *oppidum* built in a curve of the Arar river. Caesar and Ariovistus then held a parlay on horseback near the town and each general presented his position. The meeting was broken off when Ariovistus' cavalry began throwing stones at Caesar's escort. Ariovistus requested a second meeting two days later, but Caesar, doubtful of Ariovistus' intentions, sent two lower-ranking representatives instead, who were subsequently put in chains and dragged off. The affront was sufficient to set the stage for the Battle of Vosges.

Ariovistus cut off Caesar's supply lines and communications with his allies. Still, the Romans decimated the Germans, in no small part due to a charge led by Publius Crassus that broke the German line and forced them to flee. Tens of thousands of Ariovistus' men were killed and the rest – along with the rest of the Suebi who had planned to settle the area – fled by crossing the Rhine. Caesar continued the pursuit, remarkably building a bridge over the mighty river in just ten days.

The Roman campaigns continued. In 57 BC, the Nervii led a union of a dozen smaller Belgae tribes formed to defend themselves against Roman advances. Reports of the coalition worried Caesar, who raised two additional legions in Cisalpine Gaul, Legio XIII and Legio XIV, and provided Caesar with a pretext to go into battle. Despite anticipating hostilities, the initial Nervii attack surprised Caesar and Roman unpreparedness almost led to their defeat. Caesar reported that his legions' determined fighting – especially that of Legio X – and the arrival of reinforcements helped turn an embarrassing defeat into eventual victory during the Battle of the Sabis.

The Nervii lived up to their reputation for being skilled warriors willing to fight to the death. The Battle of the Sabis led to the death of the majority of their 75,000-man army. The survivors only surrendered when Caesar threatened to raze their towns. When the Belgae were subdued, their allies either surrendered or fled and Caesar was able to exploit the power vacuum to take control of a large area of northern Gaul.

By 56 BC, the Romans had been fighting in Gaul for three years and Caesar was anxious to pacify the entire region. His next campaign was against the tribes along the Atlantic seaboard. The Veneti (in today's Brittany) had pulled together a union of tribes anxious to keep the Romans out of their affairs. Campaigns along the coast required different methods of transport and supply, ones that utilized the sea. Caesar's eventual success was sufficient to build his confidence as he considered invading Britain.

But first, Caesar moved east, taking his forces across the Rhine in a campaign against the Germans. It was a punitive expedition, though the Suebi, the main target in the offensive, successfully evaded the Romans. Thereafter, Caesar returned to Brittany and led two legions across the English Channel in an exploratory expedition. Bad weather nearly led to catastrophe and precarious supply lines forced an early return, but Caesar remained undaunted and returned to Britain in 54 BC with a larger force. The Roman campaign defeated the Catuvellauni, a Celtic tribe of south-eastern Britain, who were forced into a tributary role.

Neither expedition to Britain had a lasting impact on the island, but Caesar's name was spoken throughout Rome as the greatest general of his time. Critics and political opponents, in contrast, accused him of putting personal gain above the good of the Republic. Caesar's gain – in wealth and reputation – were costly affairs for Roman coffers. Today, historians are divided. Some conclude that the pacifying of Gaul was ultimately in Rome's interest, while others declare Caesar's Gallic campaigns as pure imperialism.

Regardless of whether Caesar's actions were in the Republic's interest, the campaigns continued and the additional offensives led to the consolidation of Roman influence in Gaul. This was not without resistance, however. A significant uprising occurred during the winter of 54–53 BC, led by Ambiorix, leader of the Eburones, in north-eastern Gaul. Roman casualties were significant. The Eburones wiped out fifteen Roman cohorts at Atautuca Tungrorum and additional troops were all but eliminated at a garrison commanded by Quintus Tullius Cicero. After Caesar came to Cicero's defence, he decimated the Eburones, waging a punitive campaign against them and their allies.

Ambiorix's uprising was but a preamble to that of Vercingetorix, the chief of the Arverni in central Gaul. Vercingetorix united diverse tribes throughout Gaul and implemented a strategy that emphasized the Roman army's distance from Rome and threatened Caesar's already complex supply system. Because the Romans had repeatedly and decisively beaten the Gauls in straightforward battles, Vercingetorix studiously avoided direct, army-against-army engagements and instead concentrated on depriving the Romans of supplies. The scorched-earth strategy became Caesar's largest challenge and defeating Vercingetorix required Caesar's hurried return from Italy in order to take direct command of the army.

Avaricum (Bourges, central France), an *oppidum* in the land of the Bituriges, was spared from Vercingetorix's scorched-earth strategy as the Gauls assumed the Romans could not take it. Caesar's attempt to capture the city was among his direst moments in the Gallic campaigns. Vercingetorix refused to engage in battle yet his armies were positioned to prevent Roman resupply and even forage. Worse still, Rome's long-time allies, the Boii and the Aedui, switched sides and joined the uprising. Food was the central element of the ordeal and its scarcity led Caesar to suggest abandoning the siege. His troops refused the offer and continued the long and ultimately successful siege of Avaricum.

Vercingetorix retreated to Gergovia, and the subsequent siege of Alesia marked the final major battle of the uprising. Smaller rebellions occurred through 51 BC, but none threatened Roman control of Gaul, which remained intact until it was challenged again in the second century AD.

The Size of Caesar's Army

Before continuing beyond the Rubicon to the Civil War, it is worth pausing to determine the size of the Caesarean army. Caesar's accomplishment was greatest in Gaul, when his army was the largest and the farthest from home. To appreciate the accomplishment of feeding the Caesarean army while on campaign, one must realize that Caesar's army outnumbered all but the largest cities of the ancient world. Moving from location to location, often without predictability, Caesar not only warded off starvation among his troops, but he also nourished them sufficiently to remain an imposing fighting force. To understand just how difficult this challenge was, it is necessary to calculate the number of mouths – and maws – he had to feed. Just how big was his army?

Since the Marian reforms in 107 BC, Roman legions had a nominal strength of 6,000 to 6,200 men, a figure that was certainly higher than the fighting strength. But the sick and wounded needed to be fed as well and thus ought to be factored into the calculations.

For various reasons it makes sense to work with a figure of 5,000 men for a Caesarean legion, even though, as just mentioned, Caesar's legions were often larger. While Caesar himself did not directly mention the number of troops at his disposal, an indirect reference in Book IV of *De Bello Gallico* enables us to calculate the size of a Caesarean legion during the summer campaign in 55 BC. The context was Caesar's first invasion of Britain, which we know consisted of two legions, the VII and the X. During the return from Britain, two of the sixty-eight cargo ships used to ferry the legionaries back to Gaul became separated and were forced to land elsewhere. Caesar mentions the 'three hundred men' had to march rapidly to camp.[1] Calculating 150 men per ship for each of the sixty-eight ships, we know that the two legions Caesar brought from Britannia totalled 10,200 legionaries. From there we can determine an average legion strength of 5,100 men, undoubtedly – due to losses – smaller than the number of men he brought to Britannia. Regardless of the exact number, the size of a Caesarean legion during the summer campaign of 55 BC was a minimum of 5,000 men. Plutarch confirmed this number, stating that Caesar had with him 5,000 soldiers as well as 300 cavalry when he brought the Legio XIII to Ravenna at the beginning of the Civil War.

Feeding 5,000 men far from home would be a challenge under any circumstances, but the enormity of the task becomes clear when we consider the number of legions under Caesar's command. His army changed over the years, largely growing as the Gallic War progressed. When he commenced his operations in 58 BC, he had four legions under his command, numbered VII, VIII, IX and X. This was deemed sufficient for the defensive deployment in Cisalpine Gaul on the eve of the Gallic War, but as the deployment became more aggressive, Caesar raised and added new legions to his army. These new legions were comprised mainly of Roman citizens recruited in Cisalpine Gaul. The new legions continued the numbered sequence until his army comprised ten legions by the sixth year of the war. As the army grew, the ability to sustain it became more challenging. Still, while the number of mouths increased, so did Caesar's experience and logistical acumen.

The ten legions of at least 5,000 men – making a total of 50,000 – tells only part of the story. There were many more people involved. In 58 BC Caesar commanded light infantry, '*auxilia*', that numbered 10,000 men as well as 3,000 cavalry.[2] In addition, each legion had 700 baggage handlers and 300 muleteers. And, of course, the horses and pack animals had to be fed as well. Between 58 and 52 BC, 3,400 horses were ridden by Caesar's cavalry. After 52 BC, that number rose to 4,200. Each legion, furthermore, had 1,200 mules and the cavalry had an additional 1,200. Moreover, the legions' officers had an unknown number of other horses.

From these numbers it is possible to compute a rough estimate regarding the entirety of men and animals in Gaul. Each needed to be fed. In 58 BC, Caesar had six legions, 10,000 auxiliaries and 3,400 cavalry. The fighting force was thus approximately 43,400 men. In addition, there were 7,400 porters and muleteers, 4,000 horses and 10,560 pack animals. In 57 BC, two additional legions were added and the total of the above came to 53,400 soldiers, 9,400 handlers, 4,200 horses and 12,960 pack animals. These numbers remained largely the same until 53 BC, when the total figures jumped to 63,400 soldiers, 11,400 handlers, 4,400 horses and 15,360 pack animals. In short, the total number of people that needed to be fed was over 50,000 in 58 BC, growing to over 75,000 in 51 BC. During the same period, the number of animals grew from 14,560 to 20,800.

Astonishingly, the total number of people involved in the effort was even larger, as the figures do not include the army's officers, Caesar's personal followers, the *quaestors* and legates, or the official and private people of the army trains or operational bases. These additional numbers, though a relatively small addition, are impossible to determine for certain, but suffice it to say that many of these individuals ate significantly more and better than the soldiers. An officer's contingent could be modest or substantial. Cato the Younger, while tribune, brought fifteen slaves, two freedmen and four friends. An extreme example was Caesar's tribune Avienus during the African campaign, who required an entire cargo ship to move his entourage and belongings to Africa.[3] Cato the Elder represented the other extreme. He brought a single slave on campaign, tasked merely with carrying and preparing his food.

So, when we discuss the size of Caesar's army, we have to remember that Caesar was not merely responsible for sustaining his legionaries. In fact, at the beginning of his Gallic campaigns the number of additional men (20,800) and animals (14,560) outnumbered the number of legionaries (30,000). Putting aside the animals for the moment, the amount of food Caesar had to provide his support troops, cavalry and operating crews during the entire campaign in Gaul amounted to at least half of what he had to provide his legionaries.

The numbers, though inexact, are sufficient to show the enormity of Caesar's task. As we will see in the next chapter, individual soldiers received a ration of slightly more than 1kg of grain per day. The daily requirement of a 5,000-man legion would thus equal more than 5 tons. During the first year of the war, when Caesar had six legions under his command, more than 30 tons of grain were required. Historians have concluded that a typical two-horse Roman train wagon could carry an average of 550kg, resulting in fifty-six wagons necessary to sustain the army. As we shall also see, a normal distribution of provisions occurred at sixteen-day intervals, resulting in 82 tons per legion or, as was the case in 58 BC, 491 tons of grain for Caesar's entire army.[4]

The numbers are staggering. No general had been responsible for feeding so many men and animals so far from home. Not until modern times would it be attempted again.

The Civil War

In contrast to the Gallic War, the Civil War was fought within the Roman world. This distinction made a tremendous difference in how Caesar fed his army. In this situation, Caesar's army came into contact with individuals and peoples who were familiar with the Roman way of war. Nonetheless, logistical infrastructure – bases, supply lines – were equally important – as was securing the assistance of defeated adversaries.

Caesar's military conquests in Gaul had made him a popular hero in Rome and likely to become consul again when his governorship expired in 50 BC. The Senate, however, feared Caesar's power and popularity and ruled out the possibility of Caesar holding the office of consul for a second term. Instead, they supported Pompey as sole consul and requested that Caesar resign command of his army. Caesar, fearing prosecution and political oblivion, refused. In response, the Senate ordered Caesar to disband his army under penalty of treason.

This context explains Caesar's fateful decision on 10 January 49 BC to take his Legio XIII across the Rubicon, the shallow river that flows from the Apennine Mountains to the Adriatic Sea and marked the northern border of Italy. Because Caesar's army had officially been disbanded, his entry into Italy represented a *coup d'état*. But the action – technically an act of war on the Roman Republic – was popular, as Romans generally regarded Caesar as a hero. The die was cast.

Pompey was unaware that Caesar had crossed into Italy as commander of a single legion. He feared the march on Rome was unstoppable. Along with the consuls and much of the Senate, Pompey escaped south to Capua, allowing Caesar to enter Rome without difficulty. Pompey fled further south and the forces that were sent to engage Caesar quickly surrendered. Many of the legionaries eagerly switched to Caesar's army. Caesar then followed Pompey to Brundisium, where Pompey and his legions awaited transport to Epirus in Rome's eastern Greek provinces. Despite Caesar's entreaties that he and Pompey resume the cooperation of their earlier alliance, Pompey refused, claiming Caesar was an enemy of the state, and fleeing across the Adriatic Sea.

Caesar took full advantage of Pompey's absence from Italy. He marched north and then west, unrestricted, on a 27-day race to Hispania, where he fought Pompeian forces at the Battle of Ilerda. Caesar defeated the forces under the leadership of Lucius Afranius and Marcus Petreius, effectively bringing Roman Hispania under his control.

Caesar's next move was to assemble seven legions at Brundisium and cross the Adriatic Sea to engage Pompey in the Greek provinces. The two forces met at the Battle of Dyrrachium (today Durrës, Albania), where Caesar suffered a near-crushing defeat. Although Caesar was forced to retreat, Pompey neglected to pursue the Caesarean forces, which probably would have ended the war. Instead, Caesar was able to move south, where he established camp near Pharsalus. Pompey belatedly attacked and his troops were soundly defeated, despite superior numbers.

Pompey fled to Egypt, a move that proved fatal. Seeking sanctuary in Alexandria, he was murdered by an officer of the 13-year-old Egyptian King Ptolemy XIII, who sought good relations with Caesar. The king's action was miscalculated, however, as Caesar was enraged when Pompey's severed head was presented to him upon his arrival in Alexandria two days later. Despite being an adversary, Pompey had been a Roman consul – and had been married to Caesar's daughter. Caesar seized Alexandria and sided with Ptolemy's sister Cleopatra in the Egyptian dynastic struggle.

Caesar did not return immediately to Rome. He spent the first months of 47 BC in Egypt before moving north to Syria and then further to Pontus (northern Anatolia) in order to engage Pharnaces II, who had recently used the confusion of the Roman civil war to defeat Roman troops and gain control of the region. Pharnaces cruelly suppressed revolts in his new territories before recognizing Caesar's rapid approach from the south meant that he would have to deal again with the Romans. He disingenuously offered to submit to the Romans in a bid to delay Caesar, but the ploy failed and Caesar's army quickly disposed of Pharnaces' troops in a battle near Zela (Zile, in Turkey). It was after this skirmish that Caesar wrote to a friend in Rome, '*Veni, vidi, vici*' ('I came, I saw, I conquered').

During the period that Caesar was in Egypt and Anatolia, trouble was brewing back in Rome. Four of his legions, veterans from the Gallic War, had been stationed in Rome under the command of Mark Antony. The men grew impatient, demanding both discharge and back pay. Caesar could afford neither. He needed the troops to return to North Africa to defeat the supporters of the now-deceased Pompey and the coffers were empty. The situation deteriorated when some legionaries took matters into their own hands and ransacked estates south of Rome.

When Caesar finally returned to Rome, he addressed the legions, indicating that their disloyalty suggested that they had discharged themselves already and that he would pay them their back pay once he raised sufficient new legions to win the campaign in North Africa. Embarrassed by their mutinous behaviour, their resistance collapsed and significant numbers of legionaries agreed to stay, sufficient to form four legions for the African campaign.

Caesar's subsequent campaign in North Africa represented yet another logistical accomplishment. The key to his victory there was his defeat of the forces of Metellus Scipio, Cato the Younger and Juba at the Battle of Thapsus in 46 BC. Caesar had landed at Hadrumetum in late 47 BC eager to pursue the forces that had been loyal to Pompey. In brief skirmishes prior to the battle, two legions switched to Caesar's side. Caesar still faced 40,000 men, a significant cavalry force led by Titus Labienus, Caesar's former second-in-command during the Gallic War, and sixty war elephants. Caesar's archers attacked the elephants, which panicked and trampled their own men. After the defeat of the elephants, the Caesarean troops outmanoeuvred the opposing cavalry and destroyed their fortified camp.

After the campaign in North Africa, several Pompeian leaders, including Pompey's sons and Labienus, maintained control over significant number of troops. They escaped to Hispania, but Caesar followed and defeated the remaining opposition in the Battle of Munda in 45 BC.

During these final years of the Civil War, Caesar secured his power in Rome. His consulship was renewed twice, in 46 and 45 BC and Caesar was later proclaimed dictator for ten years, an appointment that was later amended in perpetuity. The instability led to Rome's transition from a republic to an empire and Caesar's dictatorship was too much for many. The seeds of his assassination were sown.

Honey Drink

This type of drink was known as *mulsum*. It differs from mead in that mead uses honey during the fermentation process whereas with *mulsum* the host combines the honey and wine just prior to serving. This beverage was wildly popular throughout the empire during the first century AD and was served as an aperitif at the beginning of the meal.

Ingredients:
150ml/6 fl oz honey
1 Tbsp cracked black pepper
1 tsp cracked coriander seed
1 750ml bottle of red wine

Directions:
Heat a medium-sized, dry pan over medium heat. Add the spices and toast for one to two minutes. Remove pan from stove and pour in honey. Return pot to heat and cook until fragrant. Turn off heat and stir in red wine until honey is dissolved. Pour through a strainer into a cup and enjoy.

Chapter 2

Food for Battle

Whoever does not provide for provisions and
other necessities is conquered without fighting.
Vegetius, *Epitome of Military Science.*

Perhaps the greatest testimony to Caesar's logistical genius is the paucity of evidence that any soldier under his command ever complained about his diet or rations. They complained about everything else: long marches, time away from home, cold and wet Gallic weather. But they didn't complain about food. Compare the Roman army's dietary fulfilment to that of armies – notoriously hungry groups – throughout history and Caesar's accomplishment becomes clear.

How did Caesar accomplish such satisfaction among his men? To be sure, there was an understanding of what it meant to be a Roman soldier, with clear expectations of the lifestyle, including what would be eaten and drunk; complaining about food was not part of that culture. Caesar's true accomplishment was thus his ability to meet his soldiers' expectations, including both the quantity and quality of provisions. But what exactly did Roman soldiers eat? What did they drink? What was their food for battle? And, perhaps most interesting, how did they prepare food and drink while on campaign so far from home?

Proper nutrition, of course, is necessary for any army. Caesar was not perfect and there were times in both the Gallic and Civil Wars when lack of provisions had serious deleterious effects on his men and nearly cost Caesar everything. To see the consequences of malnourishment, one need look no further than the Battle of Ilerda during the beginning of the Civil War. Caesar had just pushed his men on a gruelling 27-day march from southern Italy to the coast of Spain. During the ensuing battle, Caesar chronicled how 'the lack of grain diminished the soldiers' strength'.[1] One can imagine hunger pangs mixing with the hot summer Spanish sun to drain the army's ability to fight. Likewise, Caesar's commentary on the siege of Dyrrachium in 48 BC provides another example of military operations carried out under conditions of malnourishment. The Caesarean army was nearly wiped out, the Civil War all but lost. Caesar understood the problems that hunger created and undoubtedly knew the reason his army lived to fight another day was Pompey's ill-informed decision not to pursue his weakened enemy.[2]

Despite the disadvantageous consequences, Caesar did not avoid situations that put his soldiers at risk of diminished rations. He often raced ahead of his support system's ability to provide supplies. When he did so, he knew he was pushing the limits of a complex logistical system that had developed over centuries, a system that Caesar himself had mastered better than anyone before him. His administrative authority over supply lines and his management of requisitioning and foraging suggested that he was without peer when it came to feeding his men. Yet he placed more importance on aggressive campaigning, which he considered worth the risks incurred by stretched supply lines.

This chapter will show what the Roman soldiers ate and drank. Overwhelmingly dependent on grain for their calorific requirements, Caesar's army was typical of previous Roman armies. Grain provided sufficient calories and nutrients to anchor the Roman army's diet and it grew pervasively, both across the Republic and throughout Gaul. It could be stored in bulk for extended periods in different climates. But man cannot live on grain alone and additional foods provided sufficient nutrition to maintain Caesar's army while on campaign.

Grain

Students of Latin are often assigned Julius Caesar's *De Bello Gallico* and *De Bello Civili* long before they are proficient in the ancient language. They would be well served to be comfortable with the word '*frumentum*' and its corollaries, '*res frumentaria*' and '*frumentatio*', which serve as guide posts through Caesar's accounts of the wars. One analysis of Caesar's texts identified 156 separate usages of the term.[3]

Frumentum – most often translated as 'corn' – is the unground grain from farro, the general term referring to three types of wheat that grew ubiquitously both around the Mediterranean and in Europe north of the Alps: spelt, emmer and einkorn. *Frumentum* was hulled wheat, which means it could not be threshed; the edible grain was not separated from the chaff. It could, of course, be ground, which Roman soldiers spent a significant amount of their time doing.

The significance of the grain is that it represented 60–75 per cent of the Roman soldier's diet and it probably represented an equal percentage of calories consumed.

Regrettably – and surprisingly, considering Caesar's near-infatuation with securing corn for his troops – Caesar made no specific reference to the size of the soldiers' grain ration. In the second century BC, however, Polybius indicated that Roman 'foot soldiers generally receive in one month two-thirds of an *Attic Medimnus* of wheat'. A considerable amount of circumlocution is necessary to determine just how much two-thirds of an *Attic* was. An *Attic Medimnus*, as Polybius knew it, amounted to four-and-a-half Roman *modii*. From Polybius we turn to Plinius, who stated that a *modius* had a weight of twenty *librae*, which converts today to about a third of a kilogram.[4] So when the Ancients stated that a Roman soldier received two-thirds of an *Attic Medimnus* – or three *modii*, or sixty *librae* – of wheat per month, we can calculate that each Roman soldier received about 20kg of grain.

Historians love to argue about exactly how much Roman soldiers received, converting ancient measurements to today's, with miscalculations from ancient measuring units undoubtedly a reason for their disagreement. A. Langen, a German scholar in the nineteenth century, probably came close enough for our purposes by looking at the problem practically, asking how the grain might have been distributed. Langen determined that the daily ration, four *cotylae* (1.078 litres), roughly equalled two drinking cups that Roman soldiers carried with them. Thus, neither the soldiers nor the quartermasters needed to carry unnecessary equipment to dole out the grain. Fill the cup up twice and the rations were quickly, easily and fairly distributed.

Was this amount enough? Did it provide Roman soldiers with sufficient calories and energy? The answers require context. Cato the Elder indicated that he distributed four *modii* of wheat to his slaves in winter and four-and-a-half in summer.[5] A comparable reference by Seneca suggested that slaves received five *modii* of wheat.[6] Slaves, however, often received little else and they often had to share their food with their families. Soldiers, in contrast, generally had additional sources of calories. Since the Marian reforms in 107 BC, in fact, the commander was dependent upon his army and increasingly took into consideration the physical well-being of his soldiers.[7] In the second century AD, the historian Cassius Dio suggested Caesar understood this necessity, pacifying mutinous soldiers by reminding them that they 'satisfy [themselves] always and everywhere in sufficient amounts', suggesting that Caesar's soldiers consistently received sufficient amounts of grain.[8]

Historians know very little about Caesar's knowledge of the distribution of foodstuffs or rations. As mentioned above, he made no references to the specific amount of his soldiers' rations. Nor did he cite the intervals at which grain was distributed to the troops. He used the word '*ciberia*', the distribution of rations, just once in the context of Roman soldiers.[9] But he did make a reference that helps us infer how frequently the troops received their rations. In the first book of *De Bello Gallico*, in a description of the fifteen-day pursuit of the Helvetii, Caesar indicated that there were still two days to go until the grain had to be distributed to the soldiers.[10] That suggests that there was a regular schedule at which grain was distributed and that the interval was seventeen days.

Additional evidence comes from the *Historia Augusta*, the late Roman collection of biographies. A comment in the life of Severus Alexander indicates that seventeen days' worth of provisions was the usual amount that a fighting man was expected to carry with him. It thus seems that Caesar maintained normal distribution practices when possible.

Of course, plans are modified and abandoned during times of war. At the fateful Siege of Alesia in 52 BC, Caesar allowed for a distribution of thirty days' worth of rations so that foraging would not be necessary.[11] In practice, additional, unscheduled distributions were added after large operations[12] or when an unexpected abundance of grain presented itself.[13] During emergencies, grain gathered through immediate requisition or foraging would be distributed immediately.

In brief, a Caesarean soldier had to make his two-and-a-half '*modien*' last for sixteen days, which calculates to just over 1kg (1,022 grams) per day. Throughout the Republican period, soldiers had to pay for their grain out of their *sold*, or payment, which was actually a subsistence allowance. Caesar raised the *sold* to help soldiers alleviate the burden of paying for grain and some historians speculate that Caesar even provided the grain for free.[14]

Another aspect of the Roman army's culinary culture that we have little direct evidence about is how Caesar's soldiers prepared their rations. Caesar himself certainly never comments on the subject and other sources from the Republican period are scant. We do know, however, that their choices were limited. Specifically, they could turn their grain into porridge, bread, or a biscuit frequently known as hard tack. How they prepared their grain required significant organizational forethought and had crucial logistical and tactical implications, so the question is not trivial. Imagine, for example, the challenges involved in regularly baking bread for 50,000 soldiers. Certainly that was not possible when the army was on the move. Difficulties even arose while the legions were stationed in their winter camps.

The most common manner in which Roman soldiers ate their grain was in porridge form, which they consumed throughout both the Republican and Imperial periods. They mixed the so-called '*puls*' of ground grain, water, salt and possibly oil or fat into porridge and ate it hot or cold. The soldiers prepared the porridge themselves, of course and they could do so quickly. Porridge had the great benefit of not requiring firewood.

The second manner in which they consumed their grain was to bake it into a sort of bread using campfires. Herodian, the third century AD historian, described how the contemporary Roman emperor Caracalla prepared his food. 'He would grind enough corn for himself with his own hands and make a barley cake, which, after baking on charcoal, he would eat.'[15] Republican soldiers undoubtedly did it similarly, throwing dough on stones heated in a fire until it was baked. Consuming bread was more common at operational bases and in winter camps where providing intelligence to opposing forces was less of an issue. In the field, by contrast, firewood was not always available and lighting fires was not always permitted as it revealed positions to the enemy. Bread's primary disadvantage was that it did not keep and thus had to be eaten within days after it was prepared.

The third manner in which Roman soldiers consumed their *frumentum* was by baking it into *bucellatum*, the hard tack that frequently nourished the soldiers while on campaign. In addition to its nutritional and calorific value, *bucellatum* had a significant logistical advantage. If properly stored, it lasted for months, possibly even years. Moreover, it was versatile. It could be eaten 'straight', but it was usually soaked in water, vinegar or oil, or used as a thickener for stews, boiled together with meat and vegetables. Soldiers only ate it straight when preparing more elaborate meals was not possible.

The intrepid reader can vicariously experience the 'delicacy' of *bucellatum* by mixing four cups of wholewheat flour (or stone-ground wheatmeal) with two teaspoons of sea salt and two tablespoons of olive oil, then slowly stirring in one-and-a-half cups of water until a stiff dough results. Shape the dough into ½in thick pancakes with a 3in diameter, punch in some holes for ventilation and stick them in the oven until all the moisture has been baked out of the cakes (three hours in a 250°F oven). Once cooled, break off a piece – save your teeth by using a hammer – and enjoy. Thankfully, the reader will find a recipe for sour wine – *posca* – below to wash it down.

Hard tack, therefore, had military advantages. It could be prepared in advance of a military campaign, usually by the soldiers themselves at the *contubernium* or squad level. Moreover, the men themselves transported it without difficulty, it kept for a long time and it was readily available when fires were unwise or impossible.

But there were disadvantages as well. Most significantly, it required ovens capable of high temperatures and baking took a significant amount of time. Because of the logistical challenges of preparing hard tack, it is reasonable to assume that soldiers did not regularly consume it while they were away from operational bases. During those times, Roman soldiers settled for porridge.

In general, Roman soldiers prepared their food at the squad level, using open fires to cook meat and heat beans and lentils. Much of the reason for this decentralization was logistical. There was no centralized milling equipment, field bakery or field kitchen. Central kitchens demanded significant transportation requirements. The arrangement meant that the preparation of food was time and labour intensive. Roman soldiers carried small hand mills – '*molae manuriae*', or simply '*manuriae*' – which they transported with the pack animals. This enabled them to grind the grain into an edible form, a process that took the *contubernium* a strenuous hour or two to grind sufficient grain to last for several days. Some of the soldiers were tasked with milling and preparing the food while the rest performed other duties. In some situations, of course, the army's followers helped with the preparation of the food. Regardless, only after the grain was ground could they begin the cooking process, which, unless they were making porridge, involved open fires to heat or cook additional ingredients. If one of those additional ingredients was meat, the preparation was additionally labour intensive, unless the meat was the salted or smoked variety the soldiers received as part of their rations.

Because of its importance to the Roman diet, the grain supply was crucial. And it was immense. Caesar insisted on ever-larger stockpiles, a security that kept growing well after Caesar's death. According to Tacitus, every fort in Britain during the period 78–84 AD stored sufficient supplies to last a year. Considering that there were then 25,000 Roman soldiers in Britain and the daily ration of grain for each Roman soldier was 1.5kg per day (which translated to approximately 3,500 calories), this suggested that the daily consumption of grain was 33.5 tons.

Meat

Soldiers cannot live on grain alone, a fact as true during antiquity as it is today. Vitamins and nutrients were necessary to maintain the health of the Caesarean army. Caesar's soldiers, surprisingly, ate a relatively balanced diet, one that provided the necessary nutrients to ensure they could endure lengthy military campaigns. One significant source of nutrients came from meat. The army's reliance on *bucellatum* has led many to believe that Julius Caesar's soldiers did not eat meat, but this is patently false. While meat was certainly not a regular source of nutrition and calories, consuming it was not uncommon.

Several aspects of the army's diet suggest why so many have come to the conclusion that they did not eat meat. First, grain was actually preferred. From the commanders' perspective, farro grew everywhere, could be stored in bulk for long periods of time and was resistant to heat and cold. In short, it was logistically dependable. From the soldiers' perspective, grain could be prepared in a variety of ways while the very preparation provided a routine that gave their lives stability while they were on campaign. Obtaining meat, in contrast, was unreliable and because it spoiled quickly, it introduced the possibility of illness.

A second reason many think the Roman army eschewed meat is because Caesar repeatedly wrote that his army was upon occasion *forced* to eat meat. In one such instance in 52 BC, Vercingetorix burned down the Roman granaries and storage. The crops were not yet ripe, foraging parties were effectively wiped out or driven off and Caesar was unable to trade with nearby tribes due to the widespread Gallic uprising. Caesar wrote that the troops 'staved off the extremity of famine by driving cattle from the more distant hamlets'.[16] The men, Caesar was proud to comment, did not complain. They understood their dire situation. 'Never a word was heard from their lips unworthy of the dignity of Rome and of their previous victories. Nay more, when Caesar addressed single legions at work and declared that if the burden of scarcity were too bitter for them to bear he would raise the siege, one and all would beseech him not to do so.'[17] In addition to noting Caesar's habit of referring to himself in the third person, the reader can see that he never tired of praising his troops when it was deserved.

That same year, 52 BC, provided a second example of Caesar's army being forced to eat meat. During the famed Gallic capture of Noviodunum, the Gauls gained control of Caesar's grain storage. 'As they judged that they could not hold the town', Caesar wrote in *De Bello Gallico*, the Gauls 'set it on fire, that it might be of no service to the Romans; all the corn that they could handle at once they removed in boats, the rest they spoilt with fire and river water.' The Gauls' objective, of course, was to 'cut the Romans off from their corn supply, or to reduce them by scarcity and drive them out into the Province'. Caesar's troops, however, were able to march to the Loire, cross it and capture the enemy's unguarded cattle and grain on the other side. 'They found corn and a store of cattle and as soon as these requirements of the army had been duly supplied he decided to march into the countries of the Senones.'[18]

Throughout the Gallic War, in fact, Roman troops captured large quantities of cattle – '*pecus*'. In 54 BC, troops assaulted a stronghold of Cassivellaunus and 'found a great quantity of cattle'.[19] In the winter of 53 BC, Caesar 'concentrated the four nearest legions' and 'made a sudden and rapid advance into the borders of the Nervii', where he captured 'a great number of cattle'.[20]

These examples suggest that Roman troops were not regularly supplied with meat, but that they were not unused to it. In emergency situations, meat served as a substitute for insufficient grain. While cattle were often obtained through foraging or looting, they were, at times, undoubtedly, left to the soldiers as booty. Regardless, because meat was not part of the regular provisions, it could more accurately be described as an accidental side dish, perhaps even a desirable one that broke the monotony of grain. Caesar himself confirmed that the Roman soldiers preferred the normal grain over the indulgence of meat when he indicated that beef was a secondary ingredient that they ate to subsist.[21]

In addition, there were occasions when sufficient grain was at hand, but cattle were captured nonetheless.[22] Caesar even arranged for cattle to be supplied to his army from his allies, confirming the more or less regularity in which meat was consumed. This was not only done in times of hardship, but as a regular part of Caesar's supply system.

The consumption of meat occurred with similar regularity during the Civil War. During the Battle of Ilerda in 49 BC, Caesar found himself in a dire logistical situation. He had rushed his legions to Spain in an epic 27-day march. The local wheat was not yet ripe and the supplies of grain from the previous year had run out. Moreover, spring storms and melting snow had caused flooding, which made foraging for food all but impossible. With famine and disease striking the camp, Caesar drove Pompey's legates, Marcus Petreius and Lucius Afranius, out of their camp and restocked his army's supplies with both grain and meat.[23] Similarly, while in Dyrrachium the following year, Caesar provided his troops with meat – and vegetables and barley – in the absence of *frumentum*.

Archaeological evidence from the subsequent imperial period reveals the stunning variety of meats that supplemented the Roman troops' diet. Bones from oxen, sheep, goats, pigs, deer, wild boar and rabbits have been excavated from Roman forts in Europe and Britain. Other evidence suggests they also hunted elk, foxes, wolves, badgers and even beavers. Fish, of course, was also a common meal. The *Historia Augusta* reveals that pork was standard fare at camps,[24] whether it be cooked, roasted, boiled or made into sausages, ham or bacon. And as any ancient quartermaster would tell you, smoked or salted pork was particularly valued.

Finally, one should not forget that some animals were set aside for the *lustratio*, a sacrifice that purified the army before battle. The sacrificial animal would be cut in two and the army would march in between the halves. Generally, numerous animals were sacrificed during the *lustratio*, as evidenced by several panels of Trajan's column. While the intention was to win the favour of the gods, the ceremony also provided a significant source of fresh meat. There were times, however, when there were no animals to sacrifice. In the *lustratio* before the Battle of Philippi, shortly after Caesar's death, the former Caesarean army was compelled to divide and march between their stockpiles of wheatmeal. Apparently, this was sufficient to please the gods, as the army routed that of Brutus, leading Caesar's assassin to commit suicide.

It should be born in mind, of course, that the modern consumption of meat distorts our understanding of how much meat the ancients actually consumed. Meat simply was not a major part of the peacetime diet during the Roman Republic or Roman Empire, nor of any Mediterranean diet. Grumbling about having to eat meat was certainly due to its unpredictability and the challenges brought on by the breaking of their daily routine. The idea of meat as a fundamental component of one's diet was also considered uncouth, as testified to by Caesar's disparaging comment that the Germans 'lived on milk and flesh' alone.[25]

In all probability, the consumption of meat fluctuated, perhaps partly due to the fact that meat without firewood was useless and firewood was not always easily at hand. Still, we can conclude that meat was consumed at least semi-regularly, probably several times during a month and possibly more often.[26]

Other Foods

Other foods and ingredients rounded out the Roman soldiers' diet. Caesar mentioned salt only once in his commentaries, but the reference is telling. He instructed his camp finders to look for abundant salt supplies when searching for suitable campsites.[27] This suggests that a regular portion of salt was an important nutritional supplement. As a regular part of soldiers' provisions, salt did not just add flavouring, but provided the body with sodium, which helped with the retention of water. Interestingly, the Roman soldiers' salt ration, a *salarium*, may be the possible origin of the modern word 'salary'.

Olive oil was another ingredient that Roman soldiers consumed while on campaign. It was used for both cooking and flavouring, most commonly mixed into their grain with a pinch of salt while making their *puls*. There is overwhelming evidence, both literary and archaeological, that oil was regularly transported from the Mediterranean to northern Europe.

Legumia – legumes, often including vegetables such as beans, lentils and peas – do not seem to have been much appreciated by typical Roman soldiers. In *De Bello Gallico* they were not mentioned. The only proof that they were eaten at all is from Caesar's commentaries on the Civil War, when legumes were consumed as a substitute for grain during the siege of Dyrrachium.[28] In general, however, legumes and vegetables were not part of the Caesarean soldier's regular provisions.

Dairy products were consumed less often than one might think. They were considered the fare of less-cultured foreigners, foods that made you uncouth and possibly even sick. Caesar illustrated the Suebis' barbaric ways by including the fact that 'they make not much use of corn for food, but chiefly of milk and cattle'.[29] Caesar similarly describes the Britons in Kent living on meat and milk.[30] Caesar is also dubious of the 'fierce barbaric tribes' that survive along the Rhine by eating bird eggs.[31]

Nonetheless, the Romans did not avoid dairy entirely. Caesar reported in *De Bello Civili* that his soldiers used milk for the preparation of a substitute form of bread.[32] And the later *Historia Augusta*, though of questionable historical accuracy, lists standard camp fare (*cibus castensis*) to include cheese, whether from the milk of cows, sheep or goats, as a staple.[33] Additional evidence suggests Roman soldiers, in the Imperial period at least, made their own cheese with light and portable cheese presses.

Historians have disagreed about whether Roman soldiers ate barley (*horderum*). To be sure, barley was part of the rations for horsemen, but there is little doubt that this was meant for their horses.[34] Still, barley was consumed in emergency situations and specifically as a substitute for wheat.[35] Caesar's troops were forced to eat barley at Dyrrachium when they were blockaded by Pompey's troops.[36] Barley was also issued to soldiers as punishment. Polybius indicated commanders doled out barley to soldiers who had exhibited cowardice or committed other transgressions.[37] Not only did the punishment shame the soldiers, but barley was far less nutritious than wheat and left the soldiers hungry.[38] In a more distant example, after the battle of Cannae in 216 BC during the Second Punic War, the Senate punished the legions that refused to continue to serve by decreeing that they be placed on barley rations for seven years.[39] The men considered this to be animal fodder compared to the grain to which they were accustomed.

Two conclusions can be drawn from this overview of the military rations under Julius Caesar. First, the food was bland, making it far easier to understand the classic joke that the Roman Army conquered the world in search of condiments. The bulk of the soldiers' ration was made up of wheat, which they ate in three primary ways: most commonly, the wheat was mixed with water and possibly a little salt and olive oil into a porridge; the two alternatives were hard tack, which was baked in large quantities in ovens at stationary camps and was carried with the soldiers into the field, and bread, which was essentially dough thrown onto hot stones in fires in the field. The latter, of course, was dependent on the supply of firewood and conditions permitting the lighting of fires.

Regular rations of salt and olive oil were standard and meat, though generally not preferred, was consumed fairly regularly and probably offered a pleasant change provided the nuisance of preparing it was manageable. Beans, other vegetables and dairy products were less common but not unheard of.

The second conclusion is obvious: the rations were sufficient to sustain an army and win battles. Considering the number of miles marched in a day, day after day, and the number of battles fought, the question of how Caesar managed to provide sufficient rations becomes acute and his solutions to this challenge are rightfully to be considered some of his greatest accomplishments.

The diet of Caesar's soldiers while on campaign was limited compared to both the Roman military diet during peacetime, which included a wider variety of grains, cheese, bacon, vegetables and fresh bread, and to the legionary camps of the Imperial period, where soldiers in camps and garrisons consumed a diverse variety of meat and fish, pulses with various flavourings mixed in, beans and vegetables. Writing on wooden tablets recovered from Vindolanda, a Roman auxiliary fort just south of Hadrian's Wall in northern England, mention forty-six different types of foodstuffs. These include venison, olives, spices, honey and oysters.

Drink and Hydration

Girolamo Cardano, an Italian physician and mathematician in the sixteenth century, attributed the superiority of the Roman armies to three simple advantages. The first, obviously enough, was the ability to enlist great numbers of conscripts, which provided numerical superiority. The Romans, according to Cardano, simply overwhelmed their adversaries. The second advantage was the soldiers' strength and endurance. The Romans consistently surprised their adversaries by travelling unexpectedly long distances while carrying on their backs sufficient supplies to win battles. This strength and endurance, of course, would not have been possible without sufficient calories and nutrition. The third advantage, which Cardano understood as a physician, was the copious amount of *posca* they drank. Roman soldiers were all but limited to sour wine because a steady supply of vintage wine would have been a logistical nightmare – and because Caesar forbade his soldiers from drinking vintage wine prior to battle. Instead, they were limited to this sour wine, which was often mixed with water.

The etymology of *posca* is ambiguous. The word either derives from the Latin word *potor* (to drink) or from the Greek *epoxus* (very sharp). Regardless, *posca* was potable and its taste was indeed sharp, just as one would expect from a wine that had nearly turned to vinegar. Although there are no extent recipes for *posca*, the reader can recreate the flavour – and wash down the *bucellatum* – by boiling together one-and-a-half cups of white wine vinegar, a half-cup of honey, a tablespoon of crushed coriander seed and four cups of water. After allowing to cool to room temperature and straining the seeds, the flavour and texture will be a rough approximation of the beverage that hydrated Caesar's soldiers while on campaign. It was strong and harsh, burned the throat and was unappreciated by other cultures, who commonly referred to its severe taste. Fittingly, the sour wine offered to Jesus by a Roman soldier during the crucifixion has often been interpreted as a gesture of cruelty rather than mercy.[40]

Posca was in fact wine, but just barely. The Romans produced it by diluting vintage wine – which often turned to vinegar due to improper storage – with voluminous amounts of water and adding flavouring. Wine was a staple of Roman culture, even Roman military culture, and drinking *posca* helped the soldiers differentiate themselves from their adversaries – barbarians who drank straight water or, in the case of the Germans, massive quantities of beer. Dio Cassius wrote of the inferiority of the Britons who drank water alone and Appian claimed the Numidians were barbarians for only drinking water.[41]

33

The fact that *posca* was hardly intoxicating was an advantage, as drunkenness was frowned upon in the Roman army; Roman military culture did not condone drinking wine to excess. The consumption of wine had, on occasion, led to drunkenness. According to Plutarch, a Roman garrison in Spain in 97 BC got drunk, forgot to post a guard and was slaughtered by the Celtiberians.[42] Tacitus further reported that alcohol-sodden soldiers of the XVII Urban Cohort initiated a poorly thought-out mutiny in 60 AD.[43] The extremely low alcohol content of *posca* was thus a significant advantage.

Much has been written on the alleged health benefits of *posca*. For much of the twentieth century – and continuing today – historians have suggested that sour wine helped prevent scurvy.[44] However, *posca* contained acetic rather than ascorbic acid and therefore contained no vitamin C. It therefore was not an antiscorbutic and could not prevent scurvy. In fact, the only health benefit from *posca* was its high water content, which helped stave off dehydration, a dangerous condition of which the Romans were well aware. Appian, for example, had attributed Hannibal's defeat at Zama in part to dehydration.[45] Proper hydration, commanders knew, lengthened the range of the march and eliminated the sap of strength, agility and mental awareness in battle. Simply put, a well-hydrated soldier fights better than a dehydrated one. A secondary advantage was the fact that *posca*'s sour taste helped camouflage the bad-tasting local water throughout Gaul, the Balkans or northern Africa and thus encouraged the soldiers to drink more.

Although hydration was probably *posca*'s only health benefit, the Romans were convinced drinking wine provided other advantages. Wine was supposed to have benefits for the mind and body. Psychologically, wine was said to help cure depression, grief and memory loss. Physically, numerous digestive ailments – constipation, bloating, diarrhoea, tapeworm and urinary problems – were said to be healed by the consumption of wine. Moreover, gout, snakebites and even bad breath were treated with wine.[46]

By the second century AD, Roman gladiators were treated medicinally with wine. The Greco-Roman physician Galen of Pergamon, among the most accomplished physicians of antiquity and personal physician of Marcus Aurelius, claimed to have successfully treated gladiators' wounds with wine, boasting that not a single gladiator had died in his care. He used wine as an antiseptic for wounds and as an analgesic for surgery.

The inclusion of *posca* in the Roman army's diet predates Julius Caesar by at least 100 years. By the second century BC, soldiers and the lower classes drank it regularly. Appian included it among the provisions of Lucius Licinius Lucullus' army during the Spanish campaign of 153 BC. But its appeal apparently did not stop with soldiers and the lower classes. Plutarch wrote that Cato the Elder (234–149 BC) was quite fond of the drink. By the time of Caesar's command, sour wine was the standard drink of Roman soldiers and it became a part of a soldier's customary rations during the Roman Empire, with some generals banning the consumption of quality wine altogether, considering it to be a sign of lack of discipline. By Hadrian's time, according to the *Historia Augusta*, *posca* was part of the normal camp fare (*cibus castrensis*). Finally, a decree in 360 AD intended to further discourage the drinking of vintage wine instructed soldiers to drink *posca* on alternative days.

The near-obsession with *posca* makes one wonder if Caesar – and the Romans in general – did not ignore a valuable alternative. Namely, why didn't the Romans drink beer? It was inexpensive, more nutritious than *posca* and, provided they were not on the march, easy to brew on site.

The irony of the Roman relationship with beer is that beer had a long history around and near the Mediterranean. As early as 4000 BC, the Sumerians had developed a sophisticated beer culture, with brews made from emmer wheat and barley. Brewing traditions moved west and by 2000 BC Babylonians continued the tradition of Sumerian brewing, even regulating the practice, enabling them to codify the twenty styles of beer they brewed. One of these styles was suitable for export, which found much demand in Egypt, bringing the beverage to Rome's doorstep. Beer consumption spread so widely in ancient Egypt that it served as a commodity. Slaves, tradesmen, priests and public officials were paid in beer, which they called 'kash', the origin of the modern word 'cash'. During Caesar's time, Cleopatra understood the revenue potential for beer and established a beer tax – the world's first – that provided a constant stream into her coffers.

Yet the Romans, with noses in the air, considered beer inferior. Perhaps the fact that the Greeks, from whom the Romans took cultural clues, rejected beer led the Romans to follow suit. Yet the Greeks rejected beer for agricultural reasons: except for limited successes in Thrace, the soil and the climate were less suitable for producing grain than they were for cultivating grapes.

The Roman rejection of beer undoubtedly solidified when they began to venture into *Germania* north of the Alps, where the cultures they encountered were considered barbaric. The fact that the culture appeared to revolve around beer did not provide any impetus to imbibe in the same way. The Romans, in fact, were acquainted with the barbarians' beer drinking ways long before Caesar crossed the Alps. Marcus Porcius Cato (234–149 BC) indicated in *De Agri Cultura* that beer was the 'national drink' of the Gauls. Subsequent writers displayed a familiarity with beer and an understanding that beer had been drunk in the region for centuries. As Pliny the Elder, who had visited almost all areas of the Roman Empire, explained, 'The Gaul generally drinks "barley wine", which he has always drunk and he knows full well how to brew different styles, with which he gets inebriated'.

But the Roman historian Publius Cornelius Tacitus provides perhaps the best description of tribal German drinking habits. In *De Origine et Situ Germanorum*, which reveals much about the contact between the Romans and the Germans, Tacitus wrote that 'The Germanii serve an extract of barley and rye as a beverage that is somehow adulterated [by which he means fermented] to resemble wine'. More significant than the basic description is the contempt with which Tacitus described the Germans' constant imbibing, their ability to seek the slightest excuse for a drinking party. The Germans, he wrote, enjoyed the art of banqueting and entertaining more than any other people and it was customary for them to invite strangers into their homes to share a brew.[47]

Tacitus suggested that it would be easier to defeat the Germans by supplying them with sufficient beer. 'If we wanted to make use of their addiction to drink, by giving them as much of it as they want, we could defeat them as easily by means of this as with our weapons . . . They cultivate the grains of the field with much greater patience and perseverance than one would expect from them, in light of their customary laziness.'[48]

Cultural reasons were thus predominant in the exclusion of beer from legionaries' diets. Not only did they want to avoid behaviour similar to that of the Germans, but the link between beer and intoxication was firmly established. *Posca*, in contrast, had a very low alcohol content. Beer, though not as strong as that of today, had the ability to inebriate the imbiber when sufficient quantities were consumed.

Despite the 'prohibition' on beer, some Romans did eventually adapt the barbarian drink. A Roman merchant, who died in 260 AD in Treveris (Trier), the capital of the western part of Roman territories, was identified on his tombstone as a *cervesarius*, a beer merchant. The Roman word for beer, *cervisia*, in fact, suggests beer was a gift from the goddess of agriculture, Ceres, and that it provided strength, or *vis*.

Archaeological evidence suggests that later Romans did not merely buy and sell beer, but they brewed it as well. In 1983, a Roman brewery was discovered near Regensburg. In 179 AD, Marcus Aurelius established Castra Regina, which housed 6,000 legionaries, administrators and hangers-on. The brewery, which dates from the second or third centuries, was part of the fortification's *canaba*, a settlement for suppliers and craftsmen. The brewery contained a kiln and mash tun, a significant improvement over early German methods involving submerging half-baked loaves of bread in water. A second brewery, also discovered in the twentieth century, was located in a Roman camp near Alzey in what is now a significant wine-growing region in Rhineland-Palatinate.

Additional archaeological evidence, from Vindolanda, provides yet more evidence that the Romans had become accustomed to drinking beer after Julius Caesar's prohibition. The wooden Vindolanda Tablets suggest a regular consumption of beer: 'My fellow soldiers have no beer', wrote a Roman cavalry officer to his commander. 'Please order some to be sent.'[49] The tablets make at least two additional references to beer.[50]

But in Caesar's time, *posca* was the order of the day. Caesar's reasons were not just cultural but logistical as well. Drinking sour wine was efficient. The transportation and storage of wine was difficult and just as often as not the wine spoiled and turned to vinegar. Caesar thus had several choices: he could abandon the transportation and storage of wine, he could go to extreme measures to ensure its quality, or he could make lemonade out of lemons. The first option would have removed a defining staple of Roman culture and the second would have been a wasteful expenditure of resources. Caesar, instead, understood the benefits of *posca*. It hydrated and satisfied the Roman desire for wine – part of what made them Roman – without leading to intoxication. Soldiers often mixed their ration of sour wine with additional water in their canteens, creating a more pleasant drink and meeting their hydration needs.

Because the main ingredient of *posca* was water, the water supply was crucial and dependent upon natural circumstances. Caesar at times adjusted the length of his marches to ensure the procurement of water.[51] The location of the army's camps was also based on the condition that his army's water requirements would be met. In worse case scenarios, such as in the Alexandrian and African wars, Caesar had to fight for the water supply. As will become clear, the Roman Army's water supply presented a considerable challenge. When one considers that the daily water ration amounted to one litre of water per man and 20 litres per animal, quenching the thirst of Caesar's army while on campaign required upward of a half a million litres of water per day.

Eating Habits

Caesar's army, in typical Roman fashion, ate two meal per day, breakfast, known as the '*prandium*', and the main meal of the day, '*cena*', typically eaten one hour before curfew. (In addition, Caesar's army understood the importance of eating immediately before battle, regardless of the time of day.) The soldiers generally ate their daytime meal outside their squad tent with their *contubernium*. Evening meals were eaten inside. Because of the limitations of the fare, meals were simple and could not be compared to the elaborate *cena* for which Roman culture is so famous. Cups and bowls were earthenware and their utensils were carved out of wood. During the day, Roman soldiers generally ate standing up, with some reports of soldiers eating sitting down, as did slaves and children back in the civilian world. Commanding officers generally were at least present during the mealtimes of the soldiers, if only to test the quality and sufficiency of the food and to ensure that the quartermaster did not cheat. They rarely ate the same fare.

Some Roman legions were allowed to eat their evening meals lying down, as was typical of free Romans, but there is significant doubt cast on whether Caesar allowed the soldiers in the legions under his command to do so. Caesar had little tolerance for soldiers who dined (*epulare*) as opposed to those who took food (*cibum capare*). Plutarch described Caesar's disgust after capturing a Pompeian camp after the Battle of Pharsalus in 48 BC: 'Every tent was . . . decked out with flowered couches and tables loaded with beakers; bowls of wine were also laid out and preparation and adornment were those of men who had sacrificed and were holding festival rather than of men who were arming themselves for battle.'[52] It seems unlikely that he would have tolerated a comparable environment for his troops. He was, however, not one to let a good thing go to waste. After discovering Pompey's tent, Caesar entered it – and ate the general's dinner.[53] To the victor go the spoils.

Officers, even under Caesar's command, had different standards. While their soldiers 'took food', officers dined. And there were no iron rations for the officers, who generally found ways of obtaining 'military fine bread', which was white and less dense.[54] This should not be surprising considering officers during the Roman Republic were by and large drawn from the aristocracy. Even on campaign, most officers dined as they would at home during peacetime, complete with servants. Caesar's officers followed traditions dating back centuries. If Tacitus is to be believed, Gaius Livius, commander of Tarentum in 212 BC, started his feasts 'early in the day' and by the time 'the drinking was at its height' in the early evening Hannibal seized the town. In contrast, other officers – Cato, Scipio Aemilianus and Marius – were known to be simple eaters.[55] Regrettably, there is no direct evidence regarding how Caesar himself ate while on campaign. Circumstantial evidence would suggest he set a good example, eschewing lavish meals and avoiding habits that would diminish the respect of his men and his reporting officers.

Bucellatum

Caesar's soldiers nourished themselves with *Bucellatum*, comparable to the hard tack that has kept armies going from antiquity to modern times. It was the main source of calories for Roman soldiers on campaign. Usually eaten straight, it was also at times boiled in water to soften the biscuits or to thicken soups and stews. If it is hard and difficult to break, it has been prepared correctly.

Ingredients:
4 cups wholewheat flour or stone ground wheatmeal
2 tsp sea salt
2 Tbsp olive oil
1.5 cups water

Directions:
Mix olive oil, sea salt and flour in a mixing bowl. Slowly add water until dough is stiff. If dough sticks, add more flour.

Form into 3in squares or rounds about ⅜in to ½in thick. Place on ungreased baking sheet and poke holes in them for ventilation.

Bake at 130°C/250°F for three hours or until thoroughly dry.

Posca

Posca was made from *acetum,* a low-quality wine that had almost turned to vinegar. Spoiled wine, usually from improper storage, was also used as the main ingredient. *Posca* kept Caesar's army hydrated and its highly acidic quality killed the bacteria in local water supplies.

Ingredients:
1.5 cups red wine vinegar
0.5 cup honey
1 Tbsp crushed coriander seed
4 cups water

Directions:
Add all ingredients into a pot and boil until the honey has dissolved. Remove from heat and allow mixture to cool to room temperature. Filter the coriander seeds and enjoy.

Chapter 3

The Invention of Logistics

. . . those grievous and powerful enemies, famine and winter . . .
Plutarch, *Life of Antony*

Julius Caesar inherited a sophisticated supply capability, a system
that had continually developed throughout the Roman Republic.
In the second century BC, the Greek historian Polybius had already
acknowledged Rome's logistical ability: 'The advantages of the Romans
lay in inexhaustible supplies of provisions and men.'[1] Caesar took this
system and became the foremost executor of Rome's sophisticated
logistical capability. His ability to enhance the system in order to
maintain a sustained effort was crucial to his success. Since many of
Caesar's adversaries had given little thought to logistical support,
Caesar had a distinct advantage in combat.

Winning a war far from home is a daunting task, one that depends
on a well-developed infrastructure, an advanced economic programme
and a competent central administration. Rome was able to combine
these elements to ensure an army's supply far beyond the borders of
the Republic. Rome's administration of logistics included both central
planners as well as commanders in the field who ensured supply lines
stretched from sources of supply through operational bases all the way
to the transitory marching camps.

It is perhaps a stretch to say that Caesar invented logistics. He did,
however, understand that his army would be nothing without the
administration of supply: 'It is by proper maintenance [of supply] that
armies are kept together' he is quoted to have said.[2] Moreover, better
than anyone before him, Caesar exploited the existing infrastructure
and supply lines to feed his army.

Much of the Roman system of supply dated back to the Punic
Wars, the series of three wars fought against Carthage in the third

and second centuries BC. Supplying the armies became increasingly complex and, during the Second Punic War especially, consuls and *praetors* took on additional roles in the administration of logistics. Through a central logistical administration, the Romans successfully transported sufficient provisions from sources of supply to operational bases throughout the Mediterranean region. This system represented one prong of the Roman supply system, namely the arrangement of supplies coming from the homeland. The significance of the central administration, however, diminished in the late Republican period and this breakdown ironically benefitted Caesar as he was forced to develop the second prong of the Roman supply system, namely a stronger reliance on requisition.

The Administration of Logistics
The grain supply of the Roman army during the Republic had developed a high degree of centralization and political decision-making. When the grain supply originated from a domestic strategic base, the highest apparatus of the state was involved. The outcome of a military campaign was thus often determined long before combatants engaged. Early on, central decisions determined what happened months, even years, down the road. In order to understand the process of Roman logistics, it is helpful to consider the pre-natal stages of military campaigns.

The Senate's role in the launch of a new campaign was crucial. The body authorized the commander to engage the army in a campaign – and enlist additional troops if necessary. The Senate also voted to authorize soldiers' pay and arrange for the procurement of provisions, which would eventually feed into the Roman supply lines. This, of course, implied that the provisions could be obtained, which was no certainty. Growing, harvesting and storing grain required foresight and planning. If existing stockpiles were lacking, the grain had to be obtained from other sources.

Caesar was ultimately in charge of provisions, whether he obtained grain from strategic bases at home or through requisition. The former was wrought with politics and it was slow. From the earliest stages of the Gallic campaigns, Caesar recognized its disadvantages and he sought to circumvent the direction of the Senate, a body that was often sceptical of Caesar's actions. On the eve of the first Gallic campaign, legions under his command in Cisalpine and Transalpine Gaul had well-stocked operational bases. When the Senate authorized Caesar to lead combat operations in that area, it also authorized him to requisition supplies. He took full advantage of the opportunity and became increasingly skilled at negotiating the requisition of grain from allies and defeated foes.

One reason Caesar moved away from Rome's supply bases was that it involved the complex administration for how to pay for food and fodder. The Roman Republic had several ways of paying for the army's grain. Throughout much of the Republic, revenue was dependent on taxation. Until 167 BC, the *tributum*, a direct tax, was levied on Roman citizens to support the armies. The *tributum*, in fact, raised enough money to pay for all of the army's grain. As the provincial system developed in the late second century and early first century BC, Rome was able to collect enough revenue from the provinces that it could abolish the direct tax on Roman citizens. The Romans had successfully managed to get the provinces to pay for their wars.

In addition, the *decuma*, a grain tithe, was introduced in Sicily and Sardinia, which quickly became crucial sources of grain for the Roman army well into the period of Caesar's command. In these regions, both market purchases and forced purchases provided supplies. Allies and individuals also made contributions, though at times these were not as voluntary as the word implies. Among the allies, forced purchase, in which the buyer determined the price, became the primary means of obtaining provisions.[3]

Sources of Supply

Julius Caesar's grain supply had two main sources. The first were strategic bases in or near the Italian peninsula. As will be discussed below, Sicily and Sardinia come readily to mind. The second source of supply was through allied contributions of various sizes and arrangements. Examples of both prongs of this supply strategy can be found in earlier periods of Roman history, though no Roman commander used the combination of the two as proficiently as Caesar.

During the First Punic War (264–241 BC), the Kingdom of Syracuse on the southern tip of Sicily provided corn for the Romans when the Carthaginians cut off the Roman grain supply. Similarly, during the Second Punic War (218–201 BC), Hiero II of Syracuse again supplemented the Roman food supply. According to Livy, Hiero agreed to provision the Roman fleet and army for six months.[4]

A similar example comes from the Kingdom of Numidia on the North African coast. Numidia was also a major source of grain and it provided it to the Romans when needed during the Second Punic War. Examples of both Carthage and Numidia supplying grain to the Romans can be found during the Second Macedonian War (200–197 BC), when Roman envoys in the two states secured large quantities of grain for the Roman army: 200,000 *modii* of wheat were promised to the Roman army in Macedon and another 200,000 *modii* to be shipped to Rome. Another contribution of 200,000 *modii* was made in 198 BC.[5] Another shipment of 200,000 *modii* was shipped to the Roman army during the Third Macedonian War (171–168 BC).[6]

These examples show the large-scale contributions made to the Roman army during the conflicts of the third and second centuries BC. They are known to us because the ancient sources – Livy, in particular – drew attention to them, possibly belying the true nature of contributions made during the conflicts and setting up a false contrast between these conflicts and Caesar's during the first century BC, when smaller contributions were provided by towns and communities and used locally. Caesar emphasized these contributions, leading us to the conclusion that the Romans had moved away from the large supply operations of earlier centuries. It is also probable that Livy simply ignored the smaller contributions because, unlike Caesar, he did not think them worthy of mention.[7]

Still, there does seem to be a difference between earlier wars and Caesar's conquest of Gaul. Both undoubtedly used local allies to ensure the army's food supply, but Caesar had moved away from massive external supplies as had existed in previous centuries. We know frustratingly little about the earlier supply of Roman troops operating in the northern provinces where Caesar was appointed proconsul, Cisalpine Gaul and Narbonensis. In the centuries before Caesar, the Roman army stationed in these regions required grain and it is reasonable to assume the tithes on Sicily (and Sardinia) supplied them up until the time of Caesar's commission.

Cisalpine Gaul and Narbonensis served as a springboard for Caesar's Gallic campaigns. They became his strategic base and were there to support his conquests. Yet, in terms of the Roman army's food supply system, the base was underutilized and was not crucial to Caesar's success. Instead, the supply bases that supplied Caesar's troops came from Gaul itself, inside the areas of operation.

We can see the lack of large-scale external supplies almost from the beginning of the war, when Caesar relied to a great extent on supplies from local allies. The initial campaign against the Helvetii, in 58 BC, revealed the logistical strategy that Caesar used throughout the first years of the campaign in Gaul. The weather and time of year provided insufficient opportunities to forage and the Roman supply ships on the river Saône were unable to transport enough grain, so he cut himself loose from them and pressured his allies the Aedui to supply provisions. Roman river transport developed over the course of the Gallic War, but at the beginning it was insufficient to supply the Roman army as it conquered Gaul. Instead, contributions from allies, both forced and voluntary, were essential.

The war in Gaul was dynamic in terms of this supply system. The river network, as we shall see below, developed to the point to where goods could be delivered to all of France, a crucial development during the later years of the war when the widespread revolt under Vercingetorix deterred allied contributions and forced the Romans to rely more heavily on pillaging and plunder. The base at Narbonensis also served a valuable role later, at least when Roman legions returned there for their winter camp.

The three theatres of the Civil War – Spain, Greece and Africa – presented different situations from that of Gaul. Throughout the Civil War, Caesar had intended to use the Italian peninsula – and Sicily and Sardinia – as his strategic base. Supplies from home were to sustain his army. In each situation, however, Caesar's military strategy prevented him from fully utilizing the vast grain supplies from home.

During the first Spanish campaign, opportunity and a desire for speed led to heavy reliance on foraging and deals with allied tribes for food and fodder. The strategic base in Italy was used more for replenishment. The fact that Caesar's strategy of mobility made the strategic base useless as an immediate source of supply was characteristic of the vulnerability and limits of the resupply routes. It was faster – though certainly not more dependable – to obtain supplies locally.

In Greece, the central idea of the campaign was to occupy the Adriatic coast of Greece and drive Pompey's fleet from the area. This would free up the sea routes between Italy and the coast. Of course, there is a redundancy in the strategy in that occupying the coast would also mean capturing Pompey's well-stocked bases. The initial failures of Caesar's military offensive forced him into an area of operations that left his army in a vulnerable supply situation. In this situation, the connection to Italy would have brought him crucial advantages.

During the African campaign, Caesar found himself in the most vulnerable situation in terms of supply. His base on the North African coast was not sufficient for supplying his troops and he arranged for supplies to be brought over from Lilybaeum (Marsala) on the western-most tip of Sicily.[8] Again in this situation the supply line was less helpful than Caesar had hoped.

Although the supply lines from the strategic base during the Civil War never lived up to Caesar's expectations, the strategic base's role was more significant during this conflict than it had been during the

Gallic War. Caesar undoubtedly included it in his strategy because it lay in the centre of the theatres of war and because Caesar had unrestricted access to it.[9]

The Roman military, prior to Julius Caesar, had grown accustomed to relying on strategic bases to supply their army – or at least gave commanders the confidence that they would be able to establish a base level of supplies. Sicily and Sardinia had long been the most significant sources of supply. In the wars of the third and second centuries BC, Carthage and Numidia also became important suppliers. Although Caesar was less reliant on these provinces (especially during the Gallic War), they remained significant sources of supply. Rather than supplying the army, these supply bases became major granaries for Rome's civilian populations.

The allies, again, contributed massive amounts, as was expected of them. The Aedui, located in what is today central France, had promised grain 'as a state', implying it was expected of allies to do so. Caesar was especially incensed when grain did not arrive, especially considering that he believed the early Gallic campaigns were being fought at their behest.[10] As the Civil War undermined the central administration of the sources of supply, the allies became an increasingly important source of grain for the army under Caesar's command.

Logistical Infrastructure

The principal need behind the Roman military's development of logistics was the support of its heavy infantry legions. Marching multiple 5,000-man legions, often accompanied by a host of auxiliary light infantry and cavalry, from garrison to point of impact with the enemy was not just an exercise in tactical prowess, but a feat of both strategic and operational logistical planning and execution. Napoleonic-era French General Antoine Henri Jomini could have been talking about Roman logistics when he said: 'Logistics comprises the means and arrangements that work out the plans of strategy and tactics. Strategy decides where to act; logistics brings the troops to this point.'[11] What is relevant here is the latter part of Jomini's statement and the ability to 'bring troops' – and their food! – 'to this point' was dependent on the physical infrastructure in which Rome so heavily invested to support the expansion and control of the Republic. Recognizing the utility of a road network, complete with bridges and canals, Roman armies and their means of supply were able to traverse the better part of the European continent, through the Middle East and into Africa. This, of course, was augmented by waterborne transport that had, by the time of the late Republic, near unfettered access throughout the Mediterranean. Repeating a theme woven throughout the story of Roman logistics is that this feat is all the more impressive in that it is not only commendable by today's standards, but it was truly unrivalled in the ancient world. During a time when intra- and inter-societal travel followed along footpaths, fords and ferry points, to have a dedicated network of well-constructed and well-maintained lines of transportation afforded a decisive advantage for military operations.

At the beginning of his Gallic campaigns, a well-established network of roads stretched throughout Italy and extended into Cisalpine Gaul, where Caesar was consul. The logistical infrastructure included roads and bridges as well as water routes in the Mediterranean and along rivers. These provided the ability to move vast amounts of supplies to theatres of action. These roads, plus a web of secondary roads throughout the Mediterranean region, facilitated the supply of Caesar's army far from the Italian peninsula.

One of the most crucial factors for Julius Caesar was the transportation infrastructure in the northern Roman Republic. Infrastructure supports operational reach, one of the crucial components of strategic and tactical decision-making. The US Army speaks of operational reach in terms of the distance and duration possible for a military force to operate.[12] Specifically, operational reach can be broken down into terms of endurance, momentum and protection. But whether speaking of ancient armies or modern militaries, the increase of one element often leads to a decrease of the other two. Developments in infrastructure, however, can increase all three components and it is not surprising that Julius Caesar spent considerable effort improving the roads in Gaul, where transportation networks were less developed.

The Roman road infrastructure, in contrast to that of Gaul, was able to ensure the military's momentum while also offering protection – from attack as well as from environmental delays. Endurance on Roman roads was also less of a concern, as legions were able to maintain their speed over time by relying on trusted resting and watering sites as well as known sources of supplies.

Roman roads in the northern Italian peninsula were sufficient to project forces north into Cisalpine Gaul and the Narbonensis, but those leading into the Alps or south of them along the coast toward Iberia, were poor by Roman standards. The poor quality of the roads leading into Gaul was one of the major reasons why stockpiles of grain that came from the strategic bases in the south relied on waterways more so than overland travel. Caesar, as proconsul of Cisalpine Gaul, was responsible for maintaining – and improving – the roads and he ordered regular improvements as soon as hostilities started.

Maps were less frequently used than itineraries and the trustworthiness of the itineraries diminished the farther the traveller, whether civilian or military, went from Rome. Typical itineraries generally listed available resting, watering and animal feeding points along the route and indicated general distances between the points.

In Gaul, beyond the Roman province of Narbonensis, traders and pedestrians travelled local dirt tracks. Accompanying pack animals were generally able to navigate the tracks and some routes were able to accommodate the occasional light cart. Throughout the Gallic War, these trader tracks often became the primary routes of the Roman army. Larger-scale Gallic commerce, in contrast, moved along the many rivers of Gaul and these natural waterways influenced both the placement of roads and the locations of towns and settlements.

The network of four major waterways became major transportation corridors for Caesar's army, which used them to move men, equipment, animals and supplies throughout Gaul, even as far as the coast in preparation for the invasion of Britain.[13] The first corridor was the road that later became the Via Julia Augusta, extending from Genoa along the coast toward Iberia. The second corridor was the route that followed the Rhône River valley north through Lugdunum and along the Saône and Mosel rivers to the Rhine. This avenue cut north between the Alps and the Massif Central, establishing a link between the Mediterranean and Belgica. The convenience of water-borne traffic made this route convenient and efficient.

From this major route, roads transected Gaul toward the Atlantic Ocean. The Rhine itself curled west to the sea and roads along the riverbank were used for both foot traffic and as towpaths for animals that pulled boats along the mighty river. Parallel to the Rhine and further south, a central route passed from Durocortorum (Reims) to Gesoricum (Calais). This would have been the shortest and most direct land route to the sea. Further south still, the Romans utilized the Seine, which passed through Lutetia (Paris), to take advantage of unobstructed geographical pathways to the sea. Finally, a corridor cut between Narbo (Narbonne) to Burdigala (Bordeaux), representing the most southern route

All of these routes contained the option for water transport, at least part of the way. The waterways and tracks made Roman road building in Gaul easier and formed the skeleton of a network of roads between rivers. But as we will see below, the Romans made use of rivers whenever possible, especially for transporting supplies.

These pathways, of course, had existed for hundreds of years before the Romans arrived, making their improvement efforts easier and they continued to exist long after the Romans left, many of which formed the basis of roads that are still in use today.

Throughout the Gallic War, Caesar's army improved the existing river roads and the ways between them, which were mainly dirt tracks. After Caesar secured an area, the Roman army developed the Gallic roads in order to ensure that the legions had access to the entire region. The improved roadways gave Rome an advantage as it allowed them to manoeuvre more quickly and position troops in somewhat hostile territories, thus securing the area. Caesar's engineers rebuilt roads in the Roman style. For example, starting in 57 BC the Romans built a road that went from Cisalpine Gaul through the Great St. Bernard Pass to Geneva. In addition, engineers built causeways over wet or low ground and bridges over rivers and gullies, all with the intention of increasing mobility for soldiers and supplies.

Some bridges were temporary, such as the famous feat of constructing a bridge that crossed the Rhine near the present-day city of Coblenz in 55 BC The legions erected the bridge in just ten days, let it stand for just eighteen days – enough time for Caesar's legions to plunder the eastern shore of the river – and then promptly tore it down. (The feat was repeated in 54 BC.)

The Gallic roads, minimal though they were, supported the operational reach of Caesar's army. Yet, these roads were far more helpful during the initial conquest in Gaul than they were while consolidating the Roman gains and incorporating a subdued Gaul into the Roman Empire. While the improvement of Gallic roads, including causeways and bridges, began under Caesar's command, the construction of *true* Roman roads did not begin until after Caesar's departure from Gaul. And the difference between the Gallic and Roman roads sheds light on the limitations placed on the army under Caesar's command. In short, the Gallic roads aided the momentum of Caesar's army, but this was always at the expense of endurance and protection. As we will see below, once Caesar's legions had moved beyond the reach of the supply base of the Narbonensis, Caesar never had sufficient supplies to maintain the advantage of endurance and the lack of a reliable supply line increased the vulnerability of the troops. Because Caesar often depended on locally-obtained supplies, the momentum was often blunted by Caesar's constant need to pause before each battle or campaign in order to negotiate the supply of food with local tribes. Still, Caesar's offensive-minded temperament as a general and the military superiority of the Roman army allowed the momentum to penetrate tremendous distances, distances that the infrastructure was unable to carry over to true endurance or protection.

The physical infrastructure supported the trans-Republic operations of the legions and their requisite supply trains and the logistical infrastructure on top of it existed at the strategic level. It was multi-layered and disseminated down to the operational and even tactical level so that Rome's armies could enjoy a freedom to operate both within and outside the Republic's boundaries. Strategic logistics consisted of initiatives at the level of the Republic itself that guided overarching Roman strategies for maintaining security and control over the expanse of its territories. Logistics at the operational, or campaign, level involved tools that Roman operational planners had available when considering and planning military campaigns.

It is worth remembering that Rome was surrounded by enemies and had long borders that were not conducive to static defensive structures. This geopolitical position demanded that military planners look to other means to solve its security conundrum.[14] Rome chose to take advantage of road-reinforced interior lines and positioned its legions at strategic points that allowed them to respond to contingencies, or sally forth beyond the borders, when the situation demanded.[15] Aside from having highly-trained, well-equipped and disciplined legions at its disposal, Rome needed these legions to be mobile and also needed to ensure they stayed well fed and healthy. This required road infrastructure.

Rome's system of roads grew in line with the expansion of the Republic. The majority of the system was comprised of roads that were merely levelled earth or stabilized with gravel. More permanent, reinforced roads were located near population centres where traffic was heavier. Stone bridges along road arteries, more expedient wooden and pontoon bridges for military purposes and canals for the express purpose of military supply via ship complemented the system.[16] Where convenient, the system also made use of existing waterways. Those connected to the Mediterranean were especially valuable.[17] While this system was designed to meet military needs, either troop movement or supply, it certainly provided a secondary benefit of commercial travel.[18]

The burden of Roman road building and maintenance fell primarily on the provincial governors and the local communities. This included both the financing and the recruitment and organization of workers. The military, however, built additional roads on occasion, particularly so during wartime, and helped maintain roads during peacetime, especially those in the vicinity of its garrisons.[19]

The quality and efficacy of the transportation infrastructure is evident in the fact that much of it survives today in one form or another. Some of Rome's stone bridges still stand and are still in use. The Julian Bridge, near Bonnieux, France, was built in the first century BC to support foot and cart traffic. Today it carries pedestrians and cyclists. While many of Rome's roads have given way to 2,000 years of geological accumulation, most still exist in spirit. As Rome's roads ran in straight lines, regardless of obstacles, they often served as the most efficient routes of travel for adjoining population centres. As such, many of Europe's and the Middle East's modern highways have subsumed the Roman roads that lie forgotten below.[20]

Cartographic representations gave Rome's transportation infrastructure meaning. Caesar is credited for commissioning a number of 'world' maps that covered the entirety of Rome's breadth.[21] While these maps likely had a strategic purpose in helping the leadership of Rome better comprehend their geopolitical situation, they diverged from the more utilitarian road maps (*itineraria*), illustrated strips and land-survey maps (*formae*). While the *formae* were the detailed topographical by-product of meticulous land surveys, their scope was relatively small and their purpose was more local as they were used to detail the composition and disposition of landholdings within a colony and were often a component of the public record.[22] *Formae* served little purpose for the Caesarean-era logistician. The *itineraria*, or road maps, on the other hand, gave Rome's planners a great advantage over their adversaries.

A Roman's mental arrangement of the world was likely dominated by a sense that the known world was a collection of cities, linked by roads, with little thought to the geography in between. Roads liberated the traveller from the features of terrain and the final demarcation of the world was the edge of the Republic. Anything beyond the frontier was unworthy of cognition.[23] Within this framework the reader can understand the view of the world created by *itineraria*.

Itineraria from the early first century AD demonstrate a consistency of make-up. These simplified road maps consisted of either illustrated strips or lists of road stations. Roads on the maps linked key points of interest, demarcated by the distance in between, with no representation of the true nature of the road's path save ornamental nods to geographical features. Those features, of course, played no functional part in determining the course of one's travel. The roads and the defined waypoints provided all the information planners needed.[24] However simplified, these maps aligned with the reality of a robust road-based infrastructure. As such, *itineraria* provided the necessary details for making time-space calculations when it came to developing operational planning for matters of troop movements and logistical support.

Rome's physical infrastructure, coupled with geospatial cataloguing in the form of maps, provided military planners a significant cognitive advantage of 'world' awareness for the purposes of developing and executing operational plans. Again, it cannot be emphasized enough that Rome's adversaries lacked a system as robust and expansive as Rome's. They were more likely to have a system of local paths that were learned through experience or word of mouth. Thus, their ability to develop operational plans were limited to the scope of the individual's awareness, which had no cognitive conception of maps and pictorial representation. The existence of maps complementing the vast networks of roads gave the Romans a distinct advantage over their enemies and enabled to steady supply of provisions and materiel.

Caesar took advantage of the Roman Republic's highly developed logistical infrastructure. This complemented a central administration, which he was able to influence and sometimes circumvent, and a strategic base comprised of the granaries of Sicily, Sardinia, Carthage and Numidia. The thorough network of roads and accompanying maps provided Caesar with a better understanding of the lay of the land and what was possible logistically. All of these would be useless, however, if he had not also been a master of supply lines.

Supply Personnel and Supply Leadership

Managing the Roman army's supply system was not a one-man job, with every detail thought out by Caesar and then executed according to his commands. To some degree, everyone in the army, from the *quaestors* through the legionaries down to the *calones*, had a role to play in order to ensure everyone was fed. The supply system was complex and it is helpful to examine it from the ground up.

Every train had servants known as *calones*, who spent much of their time performing foraging duties. Caesar filled *De Bello Gallico* with examples of their activities. During operations against Ambiorix in 53 BC, Caesar sent such camp-followers to get corn in the nearest fields.[25] Against Vercingetorix the following year, Caesar sent out *calones* to forage when he would not risk sending out soldiers.[26] In a battle against the Nervii, a Belgian tribe, *calones* followed the cavalry in order to collect booty.[27] *Calones* also collected grain in the Civil War. During the Spanish campaign, Caesar sent them across the fighting area to collect food supplies.[28] In the war against Pharnaces II, the *calones* helped the Caesarean soldiers building their camps and defences.[29]

Calones were an integral part in securing the food supply and assisting the soldiers in any way they could.[30] One *calo* was assigned to every *contubernium*, so for a legion of 5,000 men and sixty centurions there would have been approximately 560 *calones*. In addition to helping the soldiers with foraging and digging trenches, they also watched the *sarcinae* – the packs the legionaries carried – during battles. In many ways the *calones* were a replacement for the slaves that the earlier armies brought with them into battle.

In addition to the *calones*, the cavalry had comparable servants. *Muliones* were muleteers, responsible for keeping the pack animals moving. In addition to driving the animals, *muliones* were assigned with organizing the transportation of the heavy packs and for caring for and feeding the animals. If a legion had approximately 1,200 pack animals, there would have been around 300 muleteers and, like *calones*, they were essentially servants who did much of the daily work of the soldiers.

The sources are frustratingly silent regarding the activities of the soldiers themselves in terms of how they received their rations. As mentioned above, they were distributed to them at intervals of about two weeks, though how this was organized is not known. Legionnaires clearly carried a portion of their rations themselves, though the exact amount is disputed. And the others? The rations may have been distributed with centurion oversight, though the *decanus* – leaders of the *contubernia* – were undoubtedly involved. Higher still, at the level of the legion, the *praefecti castrorum* – the camp prefects – and the military tribunes were contracted to distribute the grain down to the centuries. Finally, the legates conducted the supervision and monitoring of the grain supply, whether they led one or several legions.[31]

At the highest levels of Caesar's army, the role of the *quaestor* in the food supply is disputed. During the Roman Republic *quaestors* were elected public officials who supervised financial affairs in the state and its army. These key figures undoubtedly had an oversight of the food supply. In Caesar's army, however, the responsibility of the *quaestor* was fully open and the *quaestor* was regarded as the direct adjutant of the field commander and thus his actual area of responsibility was less clearly defined.[32]

We know very little about Caesar's *quaestors* in Gaul. Through the first years of the war we do not know even the name Caesar's *quaestor*, even in 55 BC, when Caesar makes reference to the 'quartermaster-general' involved with the raids on the Usipii and the Tenctari and on the first expedition to Britain.[33] Though Caesar reported conversations with them, he failed to mention their specific functions.

Caesar first mentions the name of a *quaestor* in 54 BC when discussing the dispersal of his troops to the winter camps. Marcus Crassus received command over one of the winter camps.[34] What is interesting is that Crassus' activities went well beyond food supply. One wonders when they had time to deal with their primary function. Caesar, for example, gave Crassus orders suitable for a commander, sending a messenger to him 25 miles away and bidding 'the legion start at midnight and come speedily to him. Crassus marched out on receipt of the message.'[35] Caesar 'put Crassus in charge of Samarobriva and assigned him a legion, because he purposed to leave there the baggage of the army, the hostages of the states, the public documents and all the corn which he had brought in thither to last through the winter'.[36] At the beginning of 53 BC, Crassus was still the *quaestor* at the head of the army corps in the fight against the Menapii and he had direct military orders.[37]

The next and last known *quaestor* in Gaul had similar duties. Marcus Antonius had been in Gaul since 54 BC and became *quaestor* in 52 BC at Caesar's wish. Antonius was responsible for building defences against Vercingetorix[38] and protecting baggage while legions in Belgium went off to fight.[39]

Similarly, the little we know of Caesar's *quaestors* in the Civil War suggests they also had responsibilities other than the food supply. Publius Cornelius Lentulus Marcellinus commanded a camp at Dyrrachium where the IX Legion was stationed.[40]

What these examples suggest is that Caesar's *quaestors*, the quartermasters, were possibly too busy with military activities to be responsible for the food supply. They were either positioned at the head of a legion, a winter camp, an army corps, or, in an example from the African campaign, a fleet.[41] Antonius was in command at the siege of Alesia and during all of 51 BC Lentulus Marcellinus commanded a portion of a fortification.[42]

Some historians have argued that the *quaestors* in Caesar's army were too busy with direct military activities to have sufficient oversight over the army's supply. At the very least, direct evidence of the *quaestors'* involvement in the corn supply is lacking. Caesar's references to quartermasters generally indicates they were otherwise preoccupied, often acting as commanders following Caesar's orders. During the second expedition to Britain, Crassus crossed the channel while Titus Labienus, one of Caesar's trusted lieutenants, was left on the Continent 'to ensure the corn supply'.[43] This was also true during the years 52 and 51 BC, when the military activities of the *quaestors* prevented them from being responsible for the supply. During the

54

Civil War, the *quaestor* also served as military commander while the supply functions were in the hands of two legates.[44]

So if the *quaestors* were not directly in charge of the food supply, who was? Caesar is frustratingly silent about who served in that role, writing nothing about the army leadership's role in the supply system. In a single reference in *De Bello Gallico*, Caesar described how 'the Carnutes . . . put to the sword the Roman citizens who had established themselves there for trading purposes – among them Gaius Fufius Cita, a Roman knight of distinction, who by Caesar's order was in charge of the corn supply'.[45] This was the only reference to anyone specifically commissioned with the food supply of the troops. Still, much can be drawn from it, including the significant point that Caesar appointed a private citizen as the head of his provisions system.

Gaius Fufius Cita is known because of this single citation. He was a Roman knight and in all probability a merchant, making him well suited for responsibilities dealing with supply. Because Cita was a civilian, there are limits to what we can infer about him. He did not rise through the public offices and thus it becomes difficult for us to determine his actual position, his areas of responsibility and the skills he would have developed as a public servant. He was a civilian, with no superiors other than Julius Caesar to give him orders. He was personally responsible only to Caesar as head of the supply system. But Cita's unique position reveals aspects of Caesar's thinking. Supply was clearly something Caesar valued greatly and Cita's appointment shows Caesar was willing to delegate significant portions of this area of jurisdiction to someone outside the hierarchy of public offices.[46]

Caesar's single reference to Fufius Cita reveals that he was in Cenabum, the capital of the Carnutes in present-day Orléans, a prosperous trading city located on the Loire River near the grain-rich region of Beauce. Caesar's claim that Roman citizens had 'established themselves there for trading purposes' and the vicinity of grain fields suggests the importance of the city as a collection and transhipment point for grain and explains why Fufius Cita was there. We can assume that from there Cita oversaw the resupply of grain for Caesar's troops. Nearby Agedincum (Sens) served throughout the year as a supply base and Caesar reported protecting it with two legions.[47] When that was insufficient, he sent more troops.[48] It seems logical that Caesar would maintain this supply base within easy resupply reach of the trading centre at Cenabum.

Caesar clearly did not oversee the activities of supplying grain himself and, as we have seen, it seems doubtful that the *quaestors* were involved with the responsibility. Thus it seems probably that Fufius

Cita monitored the deliveries of grain himself, either with direct orders from Caesar or with Caesar's understanding.

As we will see below, Caesar regularly concluded treaties with allies and defeated tribes for the purchase of grain. The financial aspects of such purchases would have fallen on Cita's shoulders, making him Caesar's chief buyer. The transport of the grain from the Gauls to the Roman army had to be coordinated and their execution monitored. An overview of the amounts requested and actually delivered would be required. And, of course, the constant replenishing activities had to coincide with the army's strategic planning to ensure that there was enough grain on hand to keep Caesar's legions fed, whether they were on the move or in camp. Thus, Cita was the linchpin between the supply personnel of the army's leadership and the operational base.

Fufius Cita seems to have led all activities in the operational base that related to resupplying the army. This included monitoring the delivery of grain from the Gallic allies to the Roman army. The army itself was responsible for the distribution of the rations from the operational base down to the individual soldiers. Cita was thus responsible for the entire on-going system of supply in the operational base. This reveals an insight into Caesar's thinking: he took the most important area of responsibility – the command of supply – out of the hands of aristocratic dilettantes – public officials – and put it in the hands of a private merchant whom he could trust. The *quaestor* possibly had a nominal oversight function in this capacity, though there is no evidence of this from the sources.

Caesar used private merchants throughout the Gallic campaigns and presumably throughout the Civil War as well. The Roman army needed all things imaginable: food, wagons, horses, cloth, tools. Roman traders regularly settled in the towns where Roman magazines and bases were located. These traders played an important role, gathering in such places as Noviodunum, an important storage town for Caesar. More than just hangers-on who followed the army to ply their wares, these traders helped establish the infrastructure that provided stability for Caesar's campaigns – and helped establish trading centres in Europe that survived long after the Romans were driven from the region.

1. Oysters with Sauce (see page 7).

2. Honey Drink (see page 21).

3. *Bucellatum* (see page 40).

4. Fish Cake with Fried Little Fish (see page 57).

5. Dorado Cooked in its Own Juice (see page 74).

6. Honey Pine Nut Custard (see page 100).

7. Sausages with Fried Cardoons served with Endive Salad (see pages 112–13).

8. Langoustines with Herb Sauce served with Roman Mice (see pages 124–5).

Fish Cake with Fried Little Fish

Water provided both transportation and food to the Roman Empire, so many recipes from this era include fish. The recipes of Marcus Gavius Apicius have been translated, revised and adapted from generation to generation. Different editions suggest using cuttlefish, lobster or crab, but we suggest using your favourite fillet. The salty, crunchy little fish provide a perfect complement to the creamy flavour and soft consistency of the cakes.

Ingredients:
400g / 1lb fish fillet – skinned and boned
3 egg whites
136ml / 5 fl oz cream
180g / ¾ cups all-purpose flour
Salt and pepper to taste
400g / 1lb anchovies, smelts or whitebait whole
Olive oil for deep frying

Directions:
Preheat oven to 180C / 350F / Gas 4.

Place a kettle of water over high heat. Place fish fillet in a food processor and puree until smooth. Add egg whites and puree. Add cream and puree until incorporated. Season with salt and pepper. Divide puree among 4 to 6 buttered ramekins. Place ramekins into a roasting pan. Pour hot water into the roasting pan, until it reaches halfway up the sides of the ramekins. Place the roasting pan in the oven and bake until cakes are firm to the touch, about 20 minutes. Remove pan from the oven and invert cakes onto a plate.

Pour olive oil into a pot until it reaches a depth of about 5cm / 2in and put the pot over a medium to high heat. Place flour in a plate and season liberally with salt and pepper. Dredge the small fish in the flour mixture, shake off excess flour and fry until crisp and golden brown. Drain on paper towels and season with salt immediately. Serve with the fish cake.

Makes 4 to 6 servings.

Chapter 4

Supply Lines – Definitions and Practicalities

One finds in the history books that many more armies perished
through lack of food and lack of order than through enemy action.
Cardinal Richelieu, *Testament Politique*

Sources of supply would have been meaningless without supply lines
to facilitate the movement of provisions from the strategic base to
operational bases. Rome's supply lines were the most sophisticated
logistical system in antiquity and, when combined with requisition
and foraging, they enabled Rome's military success. Caesar used
supply lines as both strategic and tactical tools. The provisions they
delivered were often more decisive than swords. As Vegetius put it in
the fourth century AD, 'Whoever does not provide for provisions and
other necessities is conquered without fighting'.[1]

With a grid of roads and waterways, lines of communication and
a cartography that put time and space in perspective for military
planners, Caesar had a firm foundation on which he could develop
a supply system for his legions. This system, based on a network of
supply points that moved the materials for war from point of origin
to the point of contact with the enemy, took into account everything
from the individual soldier's load to a tiered system of cartage. This is
not to say the system was flawless, as there were many occasions when
its capacity was overburdened or disrupted by the friction inherent
in war. Inclement weather alone often clogged the machinery of war.
Even when the system worked, requisitioning supplies from allies
and foraging in theatre were required to supplement the food shipped
from traditional sources of supply to soldiers in the field.

This chapter will look at how Rome's supply lines fed the operational bases during campaigns. Sea and river routes as well as ancient 'highways' fed operational bases, providing supplies for the trains that travelled with the legions. The soldiers themselves no doubt recognized and appreciated the fact that many foodstuffs, both massive amounts of grain and fodder as well as finer goods like wine and oil, often came from very far away.

A supply line is simply a continuous connection between a supply source and the army itself. Some historians describe Caesarean supply lines in terms of strategic, operational and tactical bases, with each type of base representing a different kind of logistical centre.[2] Strategic bases were closest to – or connected to – the sources of supply. Operational bases gathered and stored supplies in the area of operations. These were often located in ports and were large enough to hold sufficient supplies for a year. Operational bases provided stability, ensuring the army had sufficient supplies ready to be shipped to the field. From the operational base, supplies were transported to the army itself and stored in tactical bases or magazines. These were sometimes located in the army's temporary marching camp, or in a camp that had been recently abandoned. Regardless, they were always near the army. Together, the Roman transport of goods from the source of supply to the operational base and further to the tactical base represented an unparalleled logistics system.

The Punic Wars had revealed significant shortcomings in the Roman military's logistics. During the First Punic War (264–241 BC), the inability to transport sufficient grain from their strategic bases on the Italian peninsula to their soldiers in Sicily and in the western Mediterranean stymied the Romans. They eventually prevailed only after capturing grain supplies in Sicily and Sardinia. The Romans learned the benefits of regional sources of supply, which helped leaders develop a more sophisticated supply system. By the time of the Second Punic War (218–201 BC), the Romans were gathering supplies regularly from a number of regional sources and routinely moving massive quantities of provisions from them into areas of operations. By the second century BC, the improved logistical infrastructure played a key role in Rome's dramatic overseas conquests. Grain from Sicily, Sardinia, Carthage and Numidia successfully fed the Roman army throughout the Mediterranean. The improvements made as a result of these earlier weaknesses led to the sophisticated system Caesar was later able to exploit. On the eve of the Gallic War, the Roman army stationed in Cisalpine Gaul was largely supplied with grain from

Sicily and Sardinia. But Caesar knew they were insufficient to maintain fast-moving campaigns. The supply lines required to maintain his campaigns would need to be far more dynamic.

A Complex Supply System

Both the physical infrastructure and the well-developed supply lines were necessary for Caesar to move the required supplies from one end of the Republic to the other. In short, it was a multi-tiered, multifaceted system that made use of the carrying capacity afforded in everything from the individual Roman soldier, wheeled carts and wagons, beasts of burden and watercraft. Roman logisticians made use of the individual legionary, supply trains and magazines to distribute the burden of supply so that Rome's legions were ready for campaign when the call came.

From the time of Gaius Marius' military reforms, beginning with his election as consul in 107 BC, Rome's soldiers were required to be more self-reliant and as such, were forced to burden a greater portion of their individual load.[3] Aside from the iconic battle gear of a legionary, which included the chain-mail shirt (*lorica hamata*), helmet, shield (*scutum*), short sword (*gladius*), dagger (*pugio*), javelin (*pilum*) and associated leather belts and accoutrements, the legionary also carried a host of non-combat gear. Such items included a portion of the *contubernium*'s entrenching equipment (pick, axe, spade, saw and a basket), extra clothing, individual food preparation items and mess kit; all of which were affixed to a T-shaped pole with a leather satchel (together called a *sarcina*) and carried over the shoulder.

The debate around how much food the individual legionary carried is long and detailed, replete with estimates based on examples from historical texts and historical reconstruction projects under the expert guidance of archaeologists and living history enthusiasts. The existing evidence suggests that legionaries carried anywhere between three and thirty days' worth of rations. Most realistic assessments suggest they carried several days' worth on their person with the rest hauled by animals in the troop trains. This is consistent with contemporary sources and the most plausible considerations of weight and resupply needs.

Further estimates of gear carried and the associated weight of that gear, put the individual legionary's load, including grain rations, at 43kg (95lbs), with armour and equipment making up approximately two-thirds of the weight. The load of a legionary was thus eerily similar to that of today's light infantryman, moving without vehicle support for extended field operations. Differences include the fact that today's soldier only carries rations for three days, though carrying a larger portion of the unit's consumable items (batteries and crew-served weapon ammunition) easily makes up the difference.[4]

Caesar's supply was a three-tiered system that included tactical supply, tactical-operational supply and operational supply. The first tier, tactical supply, was made up of light two-wheeled carts, pack animals and wagons, which were capable of keeping pace with the marching infantrymen. This tactical supply carried the items of immediate necessity beyond those items already carried by the soldiers' individual loads. Each Roman *contubernium* consisted of eight men and had a pack animal at its disposal to carry up to 10 days of rations, the squad tent, food preparation items such as a hand mill and cooking pot, and other ancillary pieces of equipment like tools and baskets. The eighty-man century was further afforded two carts to carry artillery pieces (*carroballista*) as well as non-essential luggage. In addition, excess food rations were likely incorporated into tactical supply.

The second and third tiers of supply transported the bulk of the food and other consumable supplies. Moving from the rear headquarters to the campaigning army, the tactical-operational supply (second tier) employed carts and pack animals too, but likely had a greater proportion of wagons (and riverboats if available) to transport larger volumes of consumables, like headquarters' supplies, materials for craftsmen, replacement mounts, weapons and equipment and, at times, food and fodder. These vehicles either returned empty or served as transport for the wounded and salvaged items, like weaponry and other equipment. Available as part of the tactical-operational supply were trains for the transport of the officers and administrative equipment consisting of further tentage, servants, personal items and comfort items and trains for siege equipment, heavy tools, rope, nails and rams; these would likely be called forward if the military situation warranted their use.

The third tier, operational supply, also originating out of the rear headquarters, was comprised of heavy grain wagons and river craft detailed to carry large amounts of grain, hay and other bulk items required of troops on campaign.[5] These transports were slower and generally moved between staging points.

There were limits to the amount of supplies the Roman army could carry with it. In general, more than two weeks' worth of grain would have stressed capabilities to the limit and even that much would have been a strenuous effort. The limitations were set, above all, by the number of mules, oxen and horses, compounded by the fact that these animals also needed to be fed.

With these limitations, storage was necessary. The system developed by the Romans was a vast network of magazines set up between supply bases and the men. Close to the area of fighting, provisions could be more quickly distributed to the troops than long trains from the supply base. They had to provide storage for grain and other equipment, shelter for auxiliary personnel and animals and they had to be easily reached from established roads, navigable rivers and at times harbours. It was also common for Romans to set up magazines in established towns, preferably those that were easy to defend.

Tiered staging points, magazines, amassed supplies that supported military operations were crucial components of Rome's supply system. Magazines operated at the tactical, operational and strategic levels and consisted of tactical bases, operational bases and supply depots. The most forward of these supply points were tactical bases, positioned immediately behind the main army, often at a previously-established marching camp that the legion had vacated as it moved forward. The tactical-operational supply trains offloaded their cargo at tactical bases, unloading the items the legion might require for immediate resupply and receiving their return cargo, if any. The tactical bases might also have served as a workspace for the numerous ancillary support troops that accompanied the army – craftsmen, clerks, technicians, specialists and medical personnel.

While tactical bases would move with the army, the operational base was more of a static fixture; that said, if the situation demanded, it too could be relocated. The operational base existed as a nexus point for where strategic supply could be linked up with the tactical-operational supply trains that directly supported the army in the field. River craft could offload supplies, rear-echelon wagons could move bulk food and materials, locally-available supply and forage would be kept and troops might be stationed, either in preparation for a campaign, or in reserve. The bulk of the army's supply requirements, such as stores of grain, fodder, money, weapons, armour, remounts, timber, fabric, documents, excess personal baggage, artillery pieces, siege equipment and raw materials for craftsmen, might all be maintained at the operational base.

Unlike the operational bases, where items from various sources were received, accounted for, stockpiled and distributed as needed, supply depots served more as sequential staging points for supply items being moved from their point of origin to the tactical base. This was particularly true of inland campaigns where waterborne transport was not available. The depots served to minimize the strain on overland convoys by providing waypoints for the animals and crews to rest and resupply as they made their way to the front.[6]

Commanders knew to protect the transport of goods between the magazines and the army in the field against enemy attack and tactical decisions factored into this dimension of supply. Waterways were again preferred, but this was more of an option in Gaul than around the Mediterranean. Moreover, weather affected transporting supplies from magazine to army. Pre-Roman roads in Gaul were quickly turned to impassable mud from the slightest rain, which caused delays and potentially a breakdown of the entire system.

Whether to carry the supplies themselves or to rely on magazines was a question of priorities. At times security was the top priority, while at others flexibility was needed. The magazine system provided a high degree of security, yet dependence upon it limited the flexibility of the army. Moreover, the entire system was relatively static as the magazines took time to build and possible locations were limited due to geography and transportation issues.[7]

Sea, River and Land Transport

The Roman army preferred overseas shipment to river transport as it was cheaper and more efficient, and river transportation over land transport, which was most costly in terms of both money and effort. Still, the Roman army required all three forms of transport. Supplying the troops on campaign often began with ships travelling the open seas before supply boats navigated rivers that cut deep into territory the Romans were conquering. Land transport was unavoidable, but this often came at the end of a long journey.

The Romans regularly moved goods through the Mediterranean, across the Black Sea and along the Atlantic coast towards their areas of operation. By the first century BC, the Romans had a competent and impressive shipbuilding system and maintained a steady fleet of seaworthy vessels. Grain was the primary military provision shipped on the seas, but virtually every type of foodstuffs could be found on-board: wine, oil, salt, legumes, vegetables, meat and fish.

The Romans differentiated between routes that crossed the open sea and those that that hugged the coastlines and used different ships for each. Freighters, the large wind-powered cargo ships, were used for the former, while smaller galleys, many of which operated entirely or partly with oars, could be found within sight of shore. The large sea-going freighters were the most economical, but they were vulnerable to the key disadvantages of sea travel. Ancient sea travel, simply put, was dangerous. Freighters, less seaworthy than modern vessels, were at the mercy of the wind and weather forecasts rarely extended beyond the horizon. This danger was complicated by seasonality. In general, mid-November to mid-April presented serious challenges to overseas supply of armies. Shipping in the spring or autumn, moreover, could not be relied upon. Thus, reliable provisioning of armies was limited to the summer months.[8] Either commanders respected the impracticality of shipping supplies during the winter months, in which case the danger was mitigated, or they flirted with disaster by risking rough seas and unpredictable winds.

Of course, some commanders took more risks than others when it came to winter passages. The difference between success and failure could be dramatic and the commander had to assess whether the objective was worth the risk of losing a significant portion of a fleet filled with enough grain to supply an army through the winter. Caesar, renowned for his risk-taking, was less afraid of winter crossings than other commanders. In the middle of December 48 BC, Caesar transported five legions from Brundisium (Brindisi) to Greece across the Ionian Sea. The following year, he shipped six legions and 2,000 cavalry from Sicily to North Africa at the end of December.[9] Both examples illustrate that winter crossings were possible, although only at the risk of catastrophic loss due to bad weather or high seas.[10]

There were other disadvantages to shipment by sea. Contact with seawater spoiled foodstuffs, especially grain. The Romans generally shipped corn loose or in cloth sacks. Both methods left the grain prone to moisture and thus the development of fungi.[11] Precautions, which were never sufficient, went little beyond strategic placement on the ship. When grain was stored loose, it was at the mercy of the watertightness of the holds. A leak resulted in a wasted voyage leading to a hungry army. An additional disadvantage, of course, was the risk of hostile action by the enemy, which forced the ships to travel in a convoy or fleet or via circuitous routes.[12]

These challenges were on top of a substantial initial investment – only when a sufficient fleet to feed an army already existed did sea transport become economically viable – that made sea supply only marginally more efficient than overland travel. Some historians estimate that Caesar required between a dozen and several dozen freighters for the overseas shipment of sufficient food supplies for his armies.[13]

At the end of a successful voyage, the unloading process began as soon as the ships arrived at port. Unloading a small fleet with sufficient corn to stock a garrison for a few weeks' supply required at least a few dozen stevedores. Who these men were depended on the specific situation and could have been anyone from the *calones* that accompanied the troop trains to members of allied tribes organized to assist the

Roman supply system. The ideal situation would be for the corn to be stored in sacks small enough to be carried by individuals. Many ports were too small to handle large freighters, so the sacks would first have to be transported to smaller boats, which brought the sacks to shore. On firm ground, mules transferred the sacks to the magazines.

Caesar was well aware of the importance of harbours and he valued intelligence on their capabilities. This is clearly seen in his preparation for the first expedition to Britain. Winter was approaching, but he wanted to depart nonetheless, for little more than reasons of reconnaissance.

> He supposed that, if the season left no time for actual campaigning, it would still be of great advantage to him merely to have entered the island, observed the character of the natives and obtained some knowledge of the localities, the harbours and the landing-places. … Even traders know nothing except the seacoast and the district opposite Gaul. Therefore, although he summoned to his quarters traders from all parts, he could discover neither the size of the island … nor the harbours suitable for a number of large ships.[14]

Even earlier, in the campaign against the Veneti in 57 BC, Caesar was aware that lack of harbour intelligence could be costly. The Veneti, in turn, knew that the Romans' 'navigation was hampered by ignorance of the locality and by the scarcity of harbours and they trusted that the Roman armies would be unable to remain long in their neighbourhood by reason of the lack of corn'.[15] A similarly difficult situation arose in the Balkans during the Civil War, when Caesar had to deal with what the Romans considered to be a 'harbourless' Adriatic.

Ports often became important operational bases, with immense storage centres and suitable junctions to tactical bases down the supply line. As the supply lines continued beyond the ports, water transport was still preferred over land transport, largely because the larger bulk that could be transferred by riverboat made the whole operation more economical and navigable rivers provided quicker access into interior regions. The Rhône, for example, provided Caesar access deep into Gaul when there was sufficient – but not too much – rainfall during the Gallic campaigns. The Rhine, likewise, provided quick and reliable trade routes along the edge of Germany.

Most riverboats were 9-ton vessels, capable of carrying massive amounts of grain. Some Roman riverboats were as large as 34 metric tons. With these capacities, we can see why they were so much more economical than land transport. A single 9-ton ship could transport the same load as would require eighteen wagons or seventy-two pack animals on an overland route. Looked at another way, a single horse pulling a barge could pull 250 times the load it could carry on its back.[16] Riverboats were thus more economical, faster and required a fraction of the power than would be needed to haul the provisions over land.

This is not to say that land transport did not have its advantages. First, most major roads remained passable all year, even in rainy periods, so resupply was not limited to the summer months. Second, the grain was not at risk of spoilage by seawater. Third, the high risk of sea travel was absent and mishaps – and there were plenty – only effected a small percentage of the provisions. Significantly, overland transport also often provided the Romans with strategic advantage. Transporting supplies overland provided a much wider field of operations than coastal and river routes. In fact, the Romans regularly supplied whole armies overland for well over 100km and at times over 300km.

The main disadvantage involved with land transport was the cost of the transportation itself. Most overland shipping of supplies required draft or pack animals, which themselves needed a constant supply of fodder. In other words, the animals ate the fodder they needed to carry. This situation was compounded during desert campaigns in Africa, when massive amounts of water needed to be carried. Pack animals drank 20 litres of water per day, a significant burden to carry or pull on wagons.

Despite the hurdles involved with land transportation, it was necessary and used extensively and consistently. An army simply could not fight only along coasts and rivers. Commanders needed flexibility, without which no army can be successful.

Rainfall presented Caesar with particular challenges as it had the potential to seriously disrupt both river and land transport. Rain was predictably troublesome in spring, when the rainwater melted snows and the combined water flooded the rivers. Caesar's account of the springtime offensive in Spain in 49 BC reveals the challenges rain posed:

> A storm of such intensity sprung up that it was agreed that there had never been a greater rainfall in that district. On this occasion it washed down the snow from all the mountains, overtopped the banks of the river and in one day broke down both the bridges which C. Fabius had made. This caused serious difficulties to Caesar's army. For the camp being situated [. . .] between the two rivers Sicoris and Conga, thirty miles apart, neither of these could be crossed and they were all necessarily confined in this narrow space. The states which had entered into friendly relations with

> Caesar could not supply provisions, nor could those who had travelled some distance for forage return, being cut off by the rivers, nor could the huge supplies which were on their way from Italy and Gaul reach the camp.[17]

Because Caesar often operated at the limits of his supply system, weather had the capacity to throw a campaign in jeopardy. Flooding blocked supply routes, washed out bridges and made traditional roadways impassable. This increased significantly the length of a trip, which, in turn, increased the costs. Longer trips increased the fuel needs of men and animals, leading to a situation where both men and the animals consumed the food supplies they were meant to deliver to those fighting.[18]

Despite the challenges, the Roman army's supply lines were a remarkable achievement, unrivalled in the ancient world. But being tied to supply lines limited Caesar's freedom of movement. He recognized that the limits of supply lines created a need for local sources of food supply. How Caesar juggled the two sources of supply – the strategic bases back home and the local opportunities – was one of the fundamental factors in his success.

Operational Bases

Towards the end of long-distance transport routes, operational bases stockpiled provisions – both from strategic bases and locally-requisitioned food – to be distributed to soldiers further out in the field. Caesar, like other Roman military commanders, preferred operational bases located where water-borne supply lines linked to land routes that brought food to the army. The best example of this set-up was the operational base at Vesontio (Besançon) on the Dubis, a tributary of the Saône.

Caesar recognized Vesontio as an ideal operational base, 'for there was in that town an abundant supply of all the things needed for war and the place was so fortified by Nature as to afford great facilities for the conduct of the campaign'.[19] The river even surrounded the town on three sides like an oxbow, forming a natural moat. All of the requirements of an operational base were met perfectly. From this secure position, Caesar could undertake operations, store grain and other war materials and could care for the sick and wounded. Caesar thought so highly of Vesontio that he established his winter quarters (*hiberna*) there during the winter of 58–57 BC. During that season the river enabled the easy delivery of sufficient supplies until the next campaigning season.

Cities with existing infrastructure were also attractive locations for operational bases. During the African campaign in 46 BC, the city of Thysdrus (today El Djem, in Tunisia) acted as Caesar's operational base. Thysdrus stored enough grain to feed 40,000 men for sixty days.[20] At the operational base in Agedincum (Sens, France), one would also have found the headquarters' baggage, the army's money and documents and Caesar's personal baggage. Caesar stored all of these there, as well as weapons and armour, hostages and the army's train.[21]

The proper storage of supplies at operational bases was always a high priority. Grain and other supplies were at risk of spoilage. Caesar learned this the hard way during his African campaign, when a thunderous hailstorm destroyed a large portion of the army's grain.[22]

The *hiberna* was essentially an operational base and a typical feature of ancient military campaigns. Caesar, for example, generally did not campaign during the winter. If a campaign had not ended by the first frosts, his army bunkered down for the months of December, January and February. It should not be surprising that logistics was the primary reason for the *hiberna*. Specifically, obtaining fodder for the animals was difficult during the winter months and armies needed to remain near sizable stockpiles. Moreover, considering the amount of provisions shipped by water, one can see the challenges of transporting fodder over long distances, when sea transport was not an option due to challenging navigability during the winter months.

Although cities and towns were preferred sites for operational bases, there were few of them in Gaul, which forced Caesar to construct winter camps in a near wilderness. In these cases, much of the building materials and provisions had to be imported, with logistical decisions being made months in advance. By the end of the Gallic campaigns, Caesar's army had grown so large (ten legions) that it was often necessary to divide it and send it to several locations, each serving as a winter camp or operational base.[23]

These winter camps were also often found on or near the coast for reasons that also had largely to do with supply considerations. Stocking large supplies of grain was easier near the coast (and on navigable rivers). Moreover, should supplies run low, coastal cities and towns often had more experience with trade and buying supplies.

When you look at the various locations Caesar chose for his winter quarters during the Gallic campaigns, two significant aspects emerge. First, the winter quarters served as a supply base for the first campaigns of the summer fighting season and, second, the operational base was positioned close to the area of fighting in order to shorten supply routes.[24] In 57 BC, for example, Caesar used the operational base in the land of the Sequani in order to move out quickly into the region of the Remi and built a new operational base for the fight against the Belgae.[25]

In the winter of 55–54 BC, the *hiberna* made possible the tremendous preparations necessary for the second expedition to Britain.[26] Caesar's ships were protected in the Portius Itius (the exact location of which is still not known), which was near the shortest point of contact between the Continent and Britain. During the expedition, many of Caesar's troops remained at the operational base and prepared for the expedition's return.

The Gallic uprising in the winter of 54–53 BC wreaked havoc on the normal arrangement of both supply bases and the supply lines that fed the advanced armies. The Romans were unable to maintain steady supply bases near the fighting troops. Vercingetorix's strategy of disrupting Roman supply capability in 52 BC continued to challenge Caesar, causing him 'great difficulty in forming his plan of campaign'.[27] As Caesar noted: 'If he were to keep the legions in one place for the rest of the winter, he was afraid that the reduction of the tributaries of the Aedui would be followed by a revolt of all Gaul, on the grounds that Caesar was found to be no safeguard to his friends. If he were to bring the legions out of cantonments too soon, he was afraid that difficulties of transport would cause trouble with the corn supply.'[28] Caesar insisted that the Aedui take responsibility for resupply while also ensuring that no enemy was allowed in his rear to destroy his ability to resupply.[29] Caesar further tasked the Aedui to shore up the supply routes behind the Romans throughout the course of the year.[30]

In the absence of reliable supply bases, Caesar set up temporary tactical bases, which served primarily as protection for baggage unnecessary to wage war. One example of this occurred in early 53 BC when he sent the baggage train away for safekeeping while he moved unhindered against the Trevari and the Menapii.[31] Similarly, in the fight against the Eburones in Aduatuca, he sent the baggage of all the legions to be protected in a makeshift camp guarded by the XIV Legion.[32] Of course, such actions increased the mobility of the army, but at the expense of security.

During the first phase of the Spanish campaign during the Civil War, we see that Caesar's operational base was not suitable. It was unable to supply his troops and challenged Caesar's ability to plan larger operations. The situation improved when the Spanish tribes switched to his side, allowing him to enlarge his base and improve his supply situation. Africa presented a similar situation. He controlled only a beachhead at the beginning and he only improved the situation when he was able to bring more land under his control. Despite the improved circumstances, his supply capabilities remained limited.

Resupplying the Roman army became more difficult during the winter precisely because Caesar had to supply large numbers of men and animals in the same location for an extended period of time. But Caesar seemed to have learned from experience during the first years of the Gallic War. In the third book of De Bello Gallico, Caesar described the vulnerable winter camp (57–56 BC) established by Servius Galba in Octodurus (modern day Martigny, Switzerland) in the foothills of the Alps. Octodurus was a hamlet with a river running through the middle. Galba allowed his new Gallic allies to remain in one half of the hamlet, while he set up a fortified position, complete with ramparts and trenches, for the XII Legion in the other half. The Romans took hostages to ensure that the allies remained pacified and arrangements for corn from the surrounding area were met.[33] To Galba's horror, scouts informed him that the Gallic allies had abandoned their half of the town and had taken up positions in the higher ground above them. The grain supply had not been secured and the Gauls had cut off access for both relief and replenishments.[34]

From this experience, Caesar learned the importance of securing supplies before the legions arrived. The grain stockpiles were crucial, but so were the choice of location and the necessity of reliable supply lines that connected the winter camp to the main depots.[35] In subsequent winters, Caesar secured the grain for the winter during the preceding summer. In the fourth book of De Bello Gallico, Caesar reported that a reason for the brief initial expedition to Britain was the insufficient time required to collect grain to establish a winter camp on the island.[36] Later in Caesar's narrative, moreover, he reported that the grain he collected in Samarobriva was to last for the coming winter.[37] While Caesar was often aggressive, he learned not to take risks with provisions during the winter seasons.

The natural resources of an area were always a paramount consideration when choosing the location for a winter camp. The extent of Caesar's army required that the legions split up to different camps over the winter. He consistently reported his division of troops into several winter quarters throughout De Bello Gallico.[38] Too large a number of troops in one spot would have been too great a burden on the surrounding Gallic tribes from whom Caesar requisitioned grain. Moreover, in order to maximize the crops, the individual camps were spread over a sufficiently large area. The most extreme example was in 54 BC, when droughts caused scanty crops and the eight legions had to be distributed over a large number of states covering an area with a diameter of 150km.[39]

There is no doubt that the winter season played less of a role during the Civil War, largely due to a Mediterranean climate that was more favourable for winter campaigns. As a result, Caesar did not report on winter camps in *De Bello Civili* to the same extent that he did in *De Bello Gallico*.

Trains

We have seen how supply lines linked the sources of supply to operational bases and sometimes further to the point of contact with the enemy. Trains, in contrast, were comprised of wagons and pack animals that travelled with the army itself. There were essentially three types of trains. The first, troop trains, were relatively straightforward, containing the baggage and personal gear and the supplies of individual units. Each unit, or *contubernium*, led its own baggage and had one or two mules to carry supplies. Significantly, it is easy to see how troop trains grew in length: each century had between ten and twenty mules and each legion had hundreds, sometimes over 1,000. Of course, while mules extended the length of troop trains, they also reduced the individual legionary's burden. The second type of train, army trains, were also lengthy. They contained provisions and equipment for the force as a whole. These provisions included weaponry, workshops and building supplies. These items were sometimes shared, while others, especially weaponry, were coveted by individuals or specific units. The third type of train, officers' trains, transported the personal effects of the commanders. These could also be absurdly large. Considering what commanders brought with them, it is easy to see understand why. High-ranking officers brought with them not only their equipment, but also servants and entire households. The entourage of an officer of senatorial rank probably comprised dozens of people, often including a baker and a cook.[40] Other officers were less demanding. The Greek historian Plutarch recorded that Cato the Elder was so frugal that he travelled with a single servant while he was a junior officer and with only five servants when he was commander-in-chief in Spain (195 BC).

Caesar proved that army trains were not always necessary – an arrangement that had advantages. In 55 BC, his legions crossed over to Britain 'without baggage'.[41] Tents, provisions and tools for digging, foraging and cooking undoubtedly went with them in smaller troop trains. There were times when Caesar ordered his men to forego even those. When he and his army crossed from Sicily to Africa in 47 BC, they did so without tents or anything but the most basic of provisions.[42]

This, of course, diminished the army's fighting capacity and increased its vulnerability, but it had been a tactical decision. Too large a train restricted speed and mobility. River crossings, for example, became significantly more difficult. Trains also needed to be protected and were usually placed in the middle of the marching order with a protective screen of troops. Both Tacitus and Polybius remarked on the vulnerability of trains, with the former commenting that 'a lengthy train is easy to ambush and awkward to defend'.[43]

The size of the train would have been a tactical decision Caesar made in the field, as was expected of him. Within the area of operations, the field commander generally maintained day-to-day authority over the logistical administration. Caesar, in fact, considered it to be his duty to be responsible for issues of supply.[44]

To appreciate the size of the *impedimenta* of Caesar's legions, it is helpful to remember the load of the individual soldier. Caesar himself kept this in mind and reported frequently that soldiers carried their own packs.[45] The amount of weaponry and equipment was significant: sword, *pilum*, helmet, shield, protective slip cover, eating utensils, canteen and the rare piece of additional clothing. It is thus unlikely that they often, if ever, carried with them their entire rations. Instead, soldiers probably carried about three days' worth of grain or hard tack with them. The rest of the soldiers' personal belongings would have been carried in the trains.

Every *contubernium* had a leather tent, a stone mill, cooking utensils and other small items for daily use. For this amount of material alone, one animal was needed. And the remaining grain – 10kg per soldier after a regular distribution – would require another animal. Thus, each *contubernium* required two pack animals and each legion of 5,000 soldiers required 1,000 animals.

Extending that up to the size of the army, we see that the number of animals required were quite large: in 58 BC, Caesar's legions required some 7,200 pack animals and 1,800 muleteers. These numbers increased over the years: in 57 BC, 9,600 pack animals and 2,400 muleteers were required and after 53 BC the number swelled to 12,000 pack animals and 3,000 muleteers.

In general, the train was a challenge, but it was a necessary one. The fundamental advantage of the train was the operational independence it provided the commanders. Remaining tethered to the supply bases clearly limited mobility. Yet, the disadvantages the trains created were also significant. First, the large numbers of pack animals mentioned above required obtaining large quantities of fodder – an arduous task – and the presence of the animals limited the terrain covered to that offering fodder. Second, large trains had difficulty over rough terrain. Finally, trains were vulnerable to attack and had to be protected. It is thus not surprising that Caesar tried to limit the size of the trains as much as possible.

In his striving for mobility and independence from established routes and pathways, Caesar differentiated this organization of the trains even further. When Caesar left behind the troops' *impedimenta* in order to improve mobility, inexperienced recruits often guarded the baggage.[46] In the Civil War, Caesar often left the baggage and otherwise necessary equipment at the strategic base in order to engage the enemy as quickly as possible.[47]

Caesar acted similarly with the baggage of the headquarters. This included parts of the army's baggage, writing desks with public correspondence, offices of the *quaestors* including the public funds, and large stores of grain.[48] During campaigns Caesar often left large amounts of *impedimenta* behind, bringing with him only what was necessary for the field headquarters to function. An example of this occurred in 52 BC with the headquarters in Noviodunum.[49] Caesar brought with him six legions but left behind the heavy baggage under the protection of the recruits in Agendincum,[50] which served as Titus Labienus' operational base. Caesar stood with the remaining four legions at Lutetia Parisiorum, increasing his mobility by strictly reducing the amount of baggage he brought with him during engagements.

The situation during the Civil War was different, largely due to the fact that Caesar did not have to control large areas as he did in Gaul. Instead, speed was more important, especially in northern Spain, where his troops' manoeuvres were paramount. Caesar, simply put, often left the baggage behind.[51] During the campaigns in Greece and Africa, much of the *impedimenta* was left in Italy or Sicily, increasing both the speed with which the troops could move and to maximize the limited capacity of the ships that brought the troops into fighting zones.[52]

Dorado Cooked in its Own Juice

A dorado, *Coryphaena hippurus*, is easy to identify by its bright blue or green upper body and unusually long, golden dorsal fin, which runs nearly the length of its body. The dorado is also known as Mahi-Mahi, Golden Mackerel, or Dolphin fish. They are prolific breeders and can be found in all tropical and warm temperate seas of the world. They grow to a weight of about 80lbs/36kg, so one fish would have been able to feed several men.

Ingredients:

1 dorado fish, about 680g/1lb 8 oz, scaled and gutted and left in one piece
1 Tbsp coarse salt
1 Tbsp coriander seed
1 Tbsp olive oil
1 to 2 Tbsps red wine vinegar

Directions:

Preheat oven to 190°C/375°F/Gas 5.

Heat a large non-stick sauté pan over medium heat.

Grind coriander seeds and salt in a mortar into a course mixture. Pour onto a plate and roll the fish in the spice mixture. Season the inside of the fish as well.

Place olive oil in the sauté pan and add the fish. Cook on one side until the skin begins to brown. Flip fish to the other side and cook until the skin begins to brown. Place fish in a baking pan.

Bake, uncovered, until fish is cooked thoroughly, about 20 minutes or until the flesh feels firm. Remove from the oven, sprinkle with the vinegar and serve.

Serves 2.

Chapter 5

On the March

To distress the enemy more by famine
than the sword is a mark of consummate skill.
Vegetius, *Epitome of Military Science*

The supply lines, stretching from the source of supply through operational bases and on to tactical bases, provided the grain – the main foodstuff – for the Caesarean army. But grain alone was insufficient. Supplementing diets with local foods was a necessity and a practised habit for Caesar's troops. The Roman soldier's diet was rounded out with a system of requisition, forage and even regulated plunder and quite often Caesar's army ate meals that were both nutritionally balanced and delicious, even in the field.

The situation created a symbiotic relationship between Roman and local ingredients and diets. Imported foods influenced the surrounding eating practices and the importation of seeds and vines, as well as the desire for Roman foods. This led to the fact that the Roman military diet influenced the region in which the Romans operated more than the region influenced the Roman military diet. As with supply lines, requisition and other acquisition techniques produced problems of transportation. One of the challenges Caesar faced – a relatively good problem to have – was the question of how to carry the vast amounts of foodstuffs that could be locally found or acquired.

Marius' Mules

The heavy packs Caesar's soldiers carried were a result of the Marian Reforms, named after Gaius Marius in the late second century BC Among changes that optimized the recruitment of troops and the organization of the army, Marius codified the practice of individual soldiers carrying much of their own gear in order to reduce the size of the baggage trains and to increase the army's mobility. The soldiers carried so much on their person that they referred to themselves as 'Marius' Mules'.

Soldiers carried clothing and weapons, cooking supplies, tools and rations. The amount of rations varied, but it was rarely less than three days' worth and more commonly sufficient for up to two weeks. These items were attached to the *furca*, the bifurcated pole balanced on the soldier's shield, which was slung over the back and which distributed the weight evenly. Hung from the *furca* was a leather satchel, a cloak bag, a cooking pot, a canteen and a net bag to store foraged items. Together, these items made up the legionaries' marching pack, known as a *sarcina*. The total weight of the *sarcina* is disputed, but the most probable estimate is about 40–45kg, a considerable amount of weight considering the distances legionaries travelled.

In 1985, a German historian, Marcus Junkelmann, tested the hypothesis that this amount of weight could be carried day after day. He led a group of civilians dressed as legionaries, complete with 45kg *sarcinae*, on a 500km trek over the Alps. They successfully averaged 25km per day in replica legionary footware on their successful twenty-day trip.[1]

Caesar knew the toll such distances under heavy packs took on his soldiers. His concern was that the soldiers would be in no condition to fight after a long march and he took precautions to avoid such exhaustion. During the African campaign, Titus Labienus, who served as Caesar's second-in-command in Gaul, voiced concern that the burden of the *sarcinae* would be too much. Caesar responded by ordering a portion of the troops to travel *expediti*, without packs and ready to fight, so that they would be fresh upon arrival at the point of battle.[2] Having a force from each legion travel *expediti* was a common Caesarean tactic.

Subsequent commanders, concerned that soldiers might carry too many provisions, recognized the benefit of this Caesarean tactic. Avidius Cassius, a Roman general in the second century AD, forbade his soldiers to carry anything except bacon, hard tack and sour wine when they were on expedition. Pescennius Niger, another second-century Roman official, ordered soldiers to only eat hard tack rather than bulkier baked goods. Traditional prohibitions remained: soldiers were to abstain from drinking (vintage) wine on expedition, drinking only sour wine instead. This had as much to do with practical transportation issues as with Roman military standards.

Individual legionaries undoubtedly tried to lighten their personal load by sneaking items onto the *contubernium*'s unsuspecting mules, but these poor creatures were already weighed down with the unit's tent, the hand mills (consisting of two massive disks made of basalt), the unit's common cooking pot and tools for entrenching and foraging – axe, spade, rope, chain, saw and sickle. As stated previously, the troop trains bordered on the unwieldy. Overburdening the animals would lead to increased demand for more mules, lengthening the train further and thus defeating the purpose of the Marian Reforms.

Despite the weight that the men – and mules – carried and the size of the trains, Caesar moved his army great distances in short periods. Twenty-five kilometres per day was not uncommon. Appian, in his *Historia Romana*, testified to Caesar's 27-day march from Rome to Spain – an average of 50km per day – despite the fact that he 'was moving with a heavily-laden army'.[3] Such feats were only possible with the acquisition of local provisions.

The Marian Reforms led to ambivalent results. The movement of an entire force became more efficient and shorter trains made legions more manoeuvrable and combat-ready. However, the heavy *sarcina* weakened the Roman soldier. Tacitus noted that the Germans under Arminius could out-march the Romans, who were 'weighted down with packs and armour'.[4] Caesar's earlier solution of having a portion of his forces travel *expediti* helped the soldiers arrive fresh for battle, but not without cost. Separating too many soldiers from the trains left them vulnerable to attack. Moreover, the soldiers who had arrived at their destination unburdened found it difficult to fortify their position without the equipment from the train.[5] Travelling *expediti* was an imperfect solution, one that required the right balance.

The Marching Camp

As the Roman army left the operational base and marched toward an area of operations, it established a tactical base, comparable to the operational base, yet considerably smaller and positioned with the advanced army in the vicinity of the enemy. As the army moved forward, the tactical base followed. Previous tactical bases were either dismantled or converted into depots, which strengthened the supply line back to the operational base. Tactical bases provided the advantage of safety while the Roman army rested and nourished itself.

The renowned Roman marching camp – the tactical base – was a brilliant, well-developed campaigning technique, predating Caesar by at least 200 years. Caesar employed its use whenever his armies were outside the Republic's borders.[6] The basic idea behind the marching camp, as explained by Vegetius in the later Roman Empire, was for soldiers to provide for their own defence through the nightly construction of a palisade-reinforced earthen fortification. Deliberate attention was placed on finding a location that was both defensible and suitable for the forage of food, water and wood. Even the camp's geometry had been thought out, with both defence of the garrison and easy access to supplies outside the camp in mind. The entire facility aimed to provide tactical advantage.[7]

The marching camp, designed always as a temporary fortification, was constructed by the legion itself, or several legions in the case of larger Roman forces. While the terrain, force size and dispositions of the enemy might dictate variations in the layout, a standard template and battle drill were employed to create the camp in an expedient and orderly manner. Before the main force arrived on the site, it was preceded by a quartering (or reconnaissance) party of pioneers, designated workmen and slaves, who cleared the route, selected the camp's location and prepared it for the arrival of the main body. The standard design was that of a rectangle with rounded corners. It had four gated entrances and was surrounded by a ditch (5 to 9ft across and 3 to 7ft in depth), embankment (made up of the dirt and rocks from the ditch) and palisade (a combination of locally-found wood and pre-fashioned stakes carried by the legion). While the overall space was relative to the number of legions it garrisoned, standard design ensured that there was enough internal area to afford the living quarters (tents) with adequate stand-off, so as to not be threatened by enemy missile fire, as well as to provide manoeuvre space to prepare for battle in support of the camp's defence.[8]

When the main body of the force arrived, the *contubernia* unloaded their pioneer gear from their mules and got to work swinging their axes, spades and saws. They unloaded or prepared stakes, whether for tents or the palisade and made defensive caltrops (*tribuli*) to ward off cavalry attacks outside the camp. Repetition led to efficiency and the tasks became second nature. The ability to construct a marching camp was organic to the legion. While not every soldier was employed in building the camp, everyone had a role to play, be it guard duty, construction, fetching supplies or supervising the process. Security was emphasized as at least 20 per cent of the force was on guard at all times. More than half of the force might assume a defensive posture if the camp was being constructed while under direct threat.[9]

The time-space calculus of how a Roman force moved from camp to camp is well documented in John Peddie's *The Roman War Machine*.[10] Peddie uses Caesar's campaign in Gaul as a template for his estimations. From the time the quartering party departed from 'camp I' and arrived at 'camp II' (the new location) and began preparation it took approximately four to five hours. Construction continued as the main body of the march column arrived and continued for several more hours. The tail end of the march column, comprised of the baggage train, arrived in a newly-constructed fortified camp approximately twelve hours from the time the quartering party departed 'camp I'. Simply put, a multiple legion army could, in all likelihood, wake up, strike camp, cover 16km, rebuild the camp and be protected inside a newly-constructed fortification the next evening. This, depending on the time of year, would leave several hours for foraging.

Depending on the operational situation, the terrain and the time-related requirements of the garrison's defence, each Roman camp took on different properties. The marching camp was temporary in nature, existing for only a short duration, often less than twenty-four hours. If the nature of the campaign dictated that the camp be maintained for a longer period, then it might be gradually upgraded to a semi-permanent fortification. Essentially, defensive fortifications continued to be improved. The ditches were dug deeper, ramparts were widened, walls made higher and towers added to provide for both greater observation and to support missile/artillery emplacements. In the event that the campaign resulted in an enduring security predicament, a permanent fortification might subsume the previous camps. Permanent camps would be created to address strategic concerns, as opposed to the tactical or operation concerns that were addressed by temporary and semi-permanent camps. They served as garrisons for auxiliary units and were positioned with respect to key terrain like road junctures and waterways. These structures provided a screen of sorts and were supported by legionary fortifications that were positioned further back in Roman-controlled territory. As to be expected, these permanent camps would gradually upgrade their defensive properties through stone construction and hardened structures in lieu of wooden palisades and tentage.[11]

Since the legions did not strike all camps after their initial use, those that remained were maintained along key terrain as nexus points along the supply line. Whether in a depot capacity or an overnight staging point, the camps provided islands of refuge for stretched supply lines. Additionally, they served as waypoints for echelons of combat service support capacities. Medical personnel, craftsmen, armourers and administrators could thus be accommodated to meet the support needs of the legions on campaign. This enabled both wounded personnel to be cared for and broken equipment to be shuttled back through the supply line to be either replaced or refurbished by the appropriate craftsmen in the rear. The network of camps provided security and stability for legions beyond the borders of the Republic in that they were tied into and supported by a vast logistics network.

When describing the ideal location for encamping an army, Vegetius detailed that camps should be located near good water (and away from bad water), near plenty of forage and food and be in a position of topographical strength. That is, a camp should command the high ground and not be in terrain that is too steep or narrow that it might restrict those garrisoned inside. Caesar, furthermore, discussed the importance of forage to site selection, for (as we shall see) forage was an integral part of the supply plan. The camp was nothing less than a central point to manage foraging operations.

During Caesar's Gallic campaigns, the use of camps was primarily a defensive measure to provide security for Caesar's troops. In some instances, camps were constructed only a few miles from the enemy. This was the case when Caesar's forces tailed the Helvetii at a distance of 'no more interval than five or six miles a day' for approximately a fortnight in 58 BC.[12]

In the extreme, like during his campaign against Ariovistus in 58 BC (and later against the Belgae during the Battle of Sambre in 57 BC), camps were constructed while in contact with the enemy. That the army was often able to construct a camp while keeping an enemy at bay testifies to the numerical superiority the Roman army often enjoyed in Gaul. During the cat-and-mouse manoeuvring before battle was joined, the camps provided defensive points for a campaigning army to rest overnight and to provide a safe haven for the vast baggage trains that remained in the camp during battle.

The Battle of Vosges, also known as the Battle of Vesontio, was the final battle in the campaign against Ariovistus. It reveals how Caesar employed a series of camps tactically in both defensive and offensive manners, using the camps to both support his threatened logistics and as a riposte against the Germanic forces. The prelude to battle turned around the advance of Roman forces to correct the instable political situation through force, in the event that negotiations failed. Caesar's army advanced toward the enemy for a week, building a new camp every night and advancing further the next day. When negotiations in fact broke down, Ariovistus moved his army within six miles of Caesar's camp, halting the advance. The Suebi then repositioned themselves just two miles away from Caesar's camp in order to cut off his supply lines. Caesar attempted to bring the Germans to battle by forming up outside of his own camp every day for five days, but only succeeded in provoking cavalry skirmishes as Ariovistus kept his main army in his own camp and refused a decisive engagement. In order to alleviate the strangulation of his supply lines, Caesar sallied forth with a force of six legions plus auxiliaries and constructed a marching camp just 600 paces from the German camp. The Roman camp was constructed by a third of the troops while the other two-thirds fended off 16,000 light troops and cavalry who were threatening the endeavour. After the camp was completed, two legions and a portion of the auxiliaries remained while the rest returned to the main Roman camp. The next day Caesar again attempted to provoke an engagement by discharging the forces from their camps and forming his forces for battle. The Germans did not respond until the Roman forces retired to their respective camps. At that point Ariovistus took a portion of his force and attacked the smaller camp, but broke contact when evening came.

Having learned from German prisoners that Ariovistus was refusing battle due to the divinations of the matrons that forbade combat before the new moon, Caesar again formed for battle with the senior officers in full view of their troops. This time, however, they did not stay static. They approached the German camp, a circular laager comprised of the cartage and wagons of the German baggage train. The Germans responded by forming for battle in front of their laager, with the women and children remaining inside. Battle was joined. The Roman right flank gained the advantage, but the left began to struggle against the weight and ferocity of the German advance. Fortunately for Caesar, his quick-thinking cavalry commander, Publius Crassus, saw the predicament in the Roman battle line and took the initiative to commit the reserve, stationed in the previous marching camp, in an effort to bolster the struggling Roman left. The move proved advantageous and the Romans claimed victory. Ariovistus and his forces were routed and those that remained hurried 15 miles to cross the Rhine, leaving Gaul safely in the hands of Caesar.[13]

The Battle of Vosges shows the multifaceted nature of Roman marching camps. In addition to providing overnight security and a staging point in new locations, these camps supported the logistical efforts by serving as a point for food collection, distribution and preparation. The camps enabled safe movement during the prelude to battle, but also enabled the Romans to advance in *triplex acies*, in which two groups stood guard while the third built a new camp. Once built, the new camp housed two legions, while the other four returned to the last camp for food and rest. Their availability was the decisive factor in the victory.

It is worth noting that the concept of advancing through a series of fortified halts is still used today. While the nature of modern warfare has greatly reduced soldiers' reliance on walking and hand-to-hand combat, the idea of taking an operational pause to 'go firm' in order to rest, refit and organize staff planning is solid operational procedure. During the 2003 United States invasion of Iraq, the Marines of Regimental Combat Team (RCT) – 5, routinely took operational pauses ranging from one period of darkness to several days. One of the primary reasons was to maintain a uniformity of advance with adjacent columns as well as allow the Marines to take advantage of the temporary halt to rest and resupply. While earthen embankments and palisade fences were eschewed for two-man fighting positions dug in either by hand, or with earth-moving equipment (most often to create hull-down battle positions for armoured vehicles) and reinforced with sandbags, the idea remained the same. The military unit, in a non-permissive environment, provided its own security while on the march, so that it could best manage the friction of war.

Similar to Rome's chain of bases to support campaigns, the US military-led coalitions in Iraq and Afghanistan used a series of forward operating bases, from the division down to the platoon, to build a network of strongpoints with which to carry out the campaign. While there are obvious differences in layout and design, their functions share remarkable similarities. The establishment of networked firm bases along points of military significance, designed to allow logistics assets to traverse semi-permissive terrain from one secure base to the next and further to provide support to the forward units, remains a constant tactic.

While most notably a tactical security benefit, the Roman marching camp conferred a degree of logistical security as well. With the immediate advantage of ensuring a safe haven for the legion's baggage train and a refuge for the legion to rest and refit, a well-positioned camp enabled a legion to be sustained through local foraging opportunities and receive resupply along transportation arteries. Additionally, the same marching camp served as a nexus point for the greater supply system and in this case the marching camp conferred operational advantage. A series of camps served as waypoints for the Republic's supply system so that a legion on the march received the combat service support it required. Whether in the form of echeloned medical and maintenance support, or merely providing strongpointed supply lines, the camp system delivered to Rome's legions unparalleled logistical security.

Forage

Supplementing the food supply was a challenge. Caesar had authority over his army's logistical administration and part of that responsibility was monitoring the supply lines from the operational base to the army. He generally knew what provisions his army had, as well as what needed to be foraged, requisitioned and, when necessary, plundered. Foraging for fodder, firewood and water were routine, part of 'standard operating procedure'. Obtaining other provisions, however, took quick decision-making, often on minimal intelligence. While the sustenance of his army depended on local foodstuffs, obtaining these opened up significant security risks. These same risks applied to the enemy, however, and Caesar often used the opportunity to gain strategic and tactical advantage.

Contrary to popular belief, foraging entailed more than sending units of soldiers out with the task of returning with specific items. Small groups of soldiers did not venture out, roam the countryside and return with handfuls of berries, stolen chickens or a sack of corn. Rather, foraging was a massive undertaking, well-organized, and at times the whole army depended on its success. The size of the force Caesar sent out to forage differed depending on the hostility of the area in which the army operated, but it was always a large contingent. There were instances when Caesar sent out a single legion,[14] and others, such as during the African campaign, when he sent out several legions and light troops,[15] or two legions.[16]

Foraging required organization and planning, as well as experience and botanical knowledge. Security was necessary as was knowledge of what plants grew where. The Romans had developed a sophisticated system of foraging. The most common, which occurred on almost a daily basis, was for water, fodder and firewood. The acquisition of each of the three necessities was so common that the Romans had a different word for each: *aquari* (water), *pabulari* (fodder) and *lignari* (firewood).

Aquari was always the most immediate. Active men require two litres of water per day, an amount that pales in comparison to the needs of horses and pack animals, which required between 15 and 30 litres per day. While some militaries today are capable of flying thousands of litres of water into a foreign base on a regular basis, Caesar did not have that luxury. The location of a campsite was thus necessarily dependent upon the availability of water. If the water supply was free of enemy harassment, so much the better.[17] Caesar often lamented the fact that, for tactical reasons, camps had to be built far from water sources, a situation that required water carriers travelling long distances.[18] Worse still was when the enemy tampered with the water supply. When Curio, a general under Caesar's command, invaded Africa in 49 BC, the local inhabitants contaminated the water by throwing dead animals into the wells, resulting in widespread illness among the Caesarean soldiers.[19]

The foraging of firewood – *lignatio* –was necessary for both the preparation of meals and for warmth and illumination at night. Because each *contubernium* prepared its own meals, each needed its own fire. Thus the daily fuel requirement required constant maintenance. Caesar understood that firewood was as necessary as water, fodder or grain and insisted that sufficient levels be maintained.[20] But because its collection drained his men of energy, he commanded site planners to pick locations for camps that were near thick growths of trees whenever possible.

Of course, any action outside of the fortified camp was dangerous as the men were vulnerable to ambush, as happened to *lignatores*, foragers of firewood, while they were stocking the winter camp in 54 BC.[21] With both the necessity for the firewood and the risk of ambush high, Caesar at times assigned an entire legion to collect wood.[22]

Considering the quantities that the army's accompanying animals ate, it is not surprising that fodder, in terms of weight, was the largest requirement of the Roman army on the march. The *Historia Augusta* lists fodder first among necessary items to support the army.[23] Thus, Caesar made *pabulatio* a daily chore, even when the risk of ambush was great.[24] Horses and mules required dry fodder, such as barley or oats, to maintain their health, but this could be supplemented by grass and hay. Green fodder, in substantial quantities, was difficult to transport over long distances. Thus, it needed to be acquired on a short-term basis. After setting up the camp, hay from the surrounding areas was mowed and transported – using the very animals they intended to feed.[25] It seems the animals had to work for their food. The freshly-cut hay supplemented the feed that had been brought with the trains. In Caesar's army, it was generally the servants who carried out this task.[26] During the Civil War, the cavalry itself had to cut and gather the hay and care for the animals.

Donkeys, though less capable, had lower nutritional requirements and thus were also used as pack animals. In fact, a major military advantage of donkeys is that they can survive on low-quality food, often comprised of leaves and twigs. During the African campaign, when Pompeian troops prevented Caesar's force from foraging, donkeys were fed seaweed, washed in fresh water and mixed with grass.[27]

The need to feed the animals was so great that it often influenced the actions of armies, which often had to keep moving only because they risked exhausting the local fodder. When moving was not an option, armies were forced to stock up. Caesar ordered the collection of a thirty days' supply before the siege of Alesia in 52 BC because his army would not be able to leave.[28] During the siege of Dyrrachium (48 BC), Caesar's forces took advantage of the fact that Pompey had not stockpiled sufficient fodder and his army was unable to graze its horses or gather fodder from around the camp.[29] Caesar effectively cut off Pompey's access to supplemental animal provisions.

Security during *pabulatio* was always a priority. During the African campaign, so many enemy cavalry attacked soldiers who left the camp to gather hay that Caesar's troops had to stop altogether. In general, Caesar countered this threat by sending out foragers at different times and along different routes. He described how Vercingetorix 'kept all our foraging and corn-collecting parties under observation and when they were scattered . . . he would attack them and inflict serious loss; at the same time our men took every precaution they could think of to counteract this, by moving at uncertain times and by different routes'.[30]

The dangers involved with *pabulatio* were comparable to the foraging for food, water, or firewood. Caesar repeatedly mentioned attacks or the threat of attack on foragers.[31] Thus, cavalry almost always escorted the foragers while in enemy territory.[32] This was especially true when the foragers were forced to forage far from camp.[33] In one extreme, though perhaps not unusual, example from the expedition to Britain in 54 BC, Caesar sent three legions and the entire cavalry under the command of a legate to acquire additional feed for the animals.[34]

Caesar took the threat to foraging parties seriously and developed a sophisticated protection protocol. In enemy territory where threats were expected, the elaborate foraging force left camp in the following order: first, a part of the cavalry reconnoitred as an advance guard to the area eyed for foraging.[35] Lightly-armed soldiers, a protective vanguard, marched between the cavalry and the regular troops who came next.[36] Following the troops were train servants and the pack animals needed to haul the foraged food and fodder back to camp. Riders and lightly-armed soldiers, both of whom provided cover on the flanks, also protected the servants and animals. If the area were particularly vulnerable to attack, the guard positioned themselves in closed sections known as '*stations*' around the foragers. Ideally, scouts would also be sent out to investigate the wider surroundings. The soldiers then used their weapons to mow the grain or grass or they would plunder the houses and storage bins of the farmers. The general tactical ordering in centuries, maniples and cohorts was maintained in order to arrange themselves in their usual positions in the event of an unexpected attack.[37] After their work was done, they returned to camp in a similar formation and the grain was distributed to the soldiers and the feed to the animals.

The importance of forage in general, and *pabulatio* in particular, influenced the timing of entire campaigns. In fact, the need for fodder was a main reason why armies were forced to go into winter quarters. Caesar timed the beginning of his campaigns to correspond to the local ripening of grain. He did not join his army preparing for an expedition against the Belgae in 57 BC, for example, until sufficient forage was available in the area of operations.[38]

Foraging often led to dilemmas. During Caesar's campaign against the Helvetii in 58 BC, Caesar's problems of securing corn after the Battle of Saône became readily apparent. The Aedui, Caesar's allies whom the campaign was undertaken to support, were delinquent in providing their promised corn to Caesar's legions. The cold weather's effect on the region's agriculture complicated the situation; the corn crop was still unripe in the field and the supply of forage was insufficient. Furthermore, the requirements of the campaign forced Caesar to leave the waterborne supply lines afforded by the river Saône as he desired to maintain contact with the Helvetii. Thus corn could not be supplied via the supply lines, it could not be purchased, nor could it be taken from the field. Ultimately, just two days before the required issuing of the corn-ration to the troops, Caesar made for Bibracte, the largest and best-supplied of the Aeduan towns. This action caused the Helvetii, who suspected that the Romans faced food supply issues, to reverse their retreat and attack. The battle was fierce and long and ended with a rout of the Helvetii and the seizure of their baggage trains. A few days later the Helvetii surrendered to Caesar, marking the end of the campaign.[39]

Caesar's success depended upon the ability to live off the land, distant from operational bases. He exercised his logistical authority over all aspects of foraging with great skill, efficiency and discipline. These traits, as the historian Titus Flavius Josephus noted in the first century AD, were important elements of the Roman army's foraging operations in general: 'All their fatigue duties are performed with the same discipline, the same regard for security: the procuring of wood, food-supplies and water, as required – each party has its allotted task.'[40]

Grain was rarely, if ever, a target of forage. It came instead through the supply lines or was delivered by Gallic allies or defeated tribes. Other foodstuffs, however, were obtained from the surrounding areas. *Frumentatio* differed in significant ways from *pabulatio*. The foodstuffs gathered were often in addition to the supplies that were regularly brought by the allies or because there was an absence of regular provisions. But *frumentatio* always had specific, concrete justifications. During the first expedition to Britain, for example, the supply of grain that was destroyed in a storm was replaced by daily foraging.[41] In another example, as contributions from the Aedui decreased, Caesar nourished his entire army through foraging and captured cattle.[42]

The secondary benefit of extensive foraging was that it prevented the enemy from foraging at a later date. Caesar's soldiers harvested what was ripe and then burned, cut or trampled what had yet to ripen. Excess stores of grain were also destroyed. At times, ravaging the countryside was the primary goal, but even in those times soldiers were sure to gather whatever food, fodder or wood was needed before destroying the rest.[43]

During the final years of the Gallic War, Caesar was increasingly dependent upon foraging. Supply lines from the strategic base had broken down and contributions from allies dried up as Vercingetorix's uprising gained strength. Stores of food were a fond memory. But by then Caesar's legions had gained valuable experience and had become proficient foragers. Similarly, during the Civil War, Caesar knew he could not depend on supply lines and that deliveries from allies were not possible until victories motivated locals to switch to Caesar's side. *Frumentatio* was also not possible – and was sorely missed. In Spain, Greece and Africa, Caesar began his campaigns early in the year, making foraging difficult, if not impossible.

Caesar's enemies also understood his army was dependent on the practice. Vercingetorix, for example, exploited the Romans' dependence on foraging and incorporated counter-foraging tactics into his general strategy of defeating Caesar. At the council of Celtic leaders in 52 BC, Vercingetorix, according to Caesar, explicitly pointed out the Romans' vulnerability due to their need to forage. With their many horsemen, according to the Gallic leader, the Gauls could easily attack the foragers and disrupt the Roman food supply. Moreover, Vercingetorix spoiled the grain available to forage and laid waste to the existing food stockpiles in local magazines.

> [Vercingetorix] pointed out that the campaign must be conducted in far different fashion from hitherto. By every possible means they must endeavour to prevent the Romans from obtaining forage and supplies. The task was easy, because the Gauls had an abundance of horsemen and were assisted by the season of the year. The forage could not be cut; the enemy must of necessity scatter to seek it from

the homesteads; and all those detachments could be picked off daily by the horsemen. Moreover, for the sake of the common weal, the interests of private property must be disregarded: hamlets and homesteads must be burnt in every direction for such a distance from the route as the enemy seemed likely to penetrate in quest for forage.[44]

The Gauls executed a scorched-earth strategy in which all of the villages and farms were destroyed. Indeed, the Romans suffered heavy losses while foraging during this period and the foragers who returned to camp did so with significantly reduced amounts of food and fodder.[45]

Caesar countered by enlisting large numbers of Germanic horsemen and additional troops to serve as a protection force for the *frumentatores*. Moreover, the siege of Avaricum was also undertaken with foraging in mind, noting that it was 'situated in a most fertile district'. His army was able to take possession of huge stockpiles of food and fodder.[46] As he himself noted, Caesar 'halted at Avaricum for several days and by the immense quantity of corn and all other supplies which he found there recuperated the army after toil and want'.[47]

By the time of the Civil War, Caesar fully understood and appreciated the importance of defending his foragers and obstructing those of his enemy, practices that informed his strategy against Pompey at Dyrrachium. Encamped near Pompey's army, Caesar's army blocked Pompey's food supply while it attempted to live off the land. Caesar hoped that 'as [Pompey] had a scanty supply of provisions and had a large preponderance of cavalry, [Caesar] might be able to bring in for his army corn and stores from any direction at less risk'.[48] The plan did not work. Although many horses and pack animals perished from lack of nutrition, Pompey's soldiers were supplied from the sea while Caesar's found precious little to eat in the surrounding area.

Caesar was able to avoid disaster at Dyrrachium because he was not bound to the location. In fact, he proposed to move his camp every few days, 'to be always on the march, with the view of getting his supplies more conveniently by moving camp and visiting various places'.[49] While moving camp was possible in this situation, there were other times when it was not. When they were forced to stay in one location – during a siege for example – foragers were forced to travel greater distances to obtain food and supplies. During the African campaign in 46 BC, for example, Caesar sent his foraging parties out over a distance of 10 miles from camp and the reader senses that this was not unusual.[50] Of course, this involved great risk. Even with a protective force, such a distance prevented any chance of assistance in the event of a major attack.

In general, the military context, geography and the calendar determined the limitations of living off the land. Sustaining the army was far easier during the harvest period or immediately thereafter. Unharvested ripe crops were also suitable. During the winter and spring, food had to be plundered, stolen or bartered from civilian stores in towns or in the countryside. Fortified towns, of course, made this a challenging enterprise. When food sources were scarce, foraging parties had to travel great distances and they had to seek in isolated, less fruitful locations.

Because of the unpredictability of forage, commanders far preferred organized, dependable provisioning. The interplay of logistical security and operational flexibility was always the commanders' central equation. When the security of organized supply was not available, they embraced the flexibility provided by living off the land.

Requisitioning

Vegetius remarked that a commander must make an exact count of the number of troops to be used in an operation and the expenses of maintaining them, 'so that the provinces may in plenty of time furnish the forage, corn and all other kinds of provisions demanded of them to be transported . . . and gathered into the strongest and most convenient cities before the opening of the campaign'.[51] This method of provincial supply through direct negotiation with the provinces and allies became an increasingly important method of supply during the late Republic.[52] Caesar depended on it, calling on allies and adjacent provinces to support his legions during both the Gallic Wars and the Civil War. In preparation for his offensive against Ariovistus and the Suebi in 58 BC, Caesar made it known that his previous corn-supply woes during the campaign against the Helvetii were no longer a concern. He remarked, 'Corn is being supplied by the Sequani, the Leuci and the Lingones, and the corn crops in the fields are already ripe'.[53] Whenever possible, Caesar negotiated and amassed stores of excess corn and grain in towns, using them to serve as supply waypoints.

Requisitioning, obtaining supplies from allies and defeated foes, was far safer than forage. Because of the usual power imbalance between the Romans and their allies or former belligerents, requisition often entailed the forced purchase of goods. Rome's armies often demanded the vanquished surrender provisions, usually in corn.[54] Providing grain to the Caesarean army was a usual part of surrender. During his second expedition to Britain in 54 BC, for example, the Trinobantes, one of the more powerful tribes in south-eastern Britain, sued for peace. Caesar required of them corn for his army and forty hostages to ensure its delivery; they complied without delay.[55] Requisitioning either entailed an involuntary seizure or a 'forced' purchase. Because Caesar generally sought good relations in the areas he occupied, however, the Romans often paid for the food.

The first reference to requisition is found early in *De Bello Gallico*, as Caesar reported his first contacts with the enemy. The Helvetii, having departed their lands, threatened to cross Roman borders. The act threatened to unsettle the peace that had been established between the Romans and their neighbours. During their transit, the Helvetii had plundered Aedui villages and refused to make peace with the Romans. Caesar could not tolerate the actions of the Helvetii and had made an arrangement with the Aedui. 'Caesar was daily pressing the Aedui for the corn that they promised as a state.'[56] The details of the arrangement are lost, but the reference becomes clear once the pattern of Caesar's requisition system was employed throughout the Gallic campaigns and continued with some variation during the Civil War.

The Aedui's promises of corn reveal a major component of Caesar's supply system. Because supply lines had a definite limit, he depended on requisition from allied or defeated tribes to supply his troops while on foreign soil. Narbonensis, the Roman province that served as the supply base for Caesar's troops in Cisalpine and Transalpine Gaul, was less effective supporting Roman troops further north, especially north of the Alps.

While the Romans had followed the Helvetii along the Saône, the supply had been delivered via the Rhône. It is likely that this was the only time throughout the Gallic War that the grain for the entire Caesarean army was procured in Roman territories and delivered to Roman troops. As the Helvetian forces moved away from the Saône, Caesar was forced to separate from the supply lines. 'He was less able to use the corn-supply that he had brought up the river Saône in boats and he did not wish to lose touch with the Helvetii.'[57] Travel over land and paths, however, proved too much for Roman supply lines and Caesar could not obtain the 31 tons of grain needed for his six legions. These severe limitations placed on Roman supply by land travel forced Caesar to an arrangement with the Aedui.

Still, difficulties arose. The Aedui were unable to supply the necessary grain. 'For by reason of cold weather . . . not only were the corn crops in the fields unripe, but there was not even a sufficient supply of forage to be had.'[58] Thus, Caesar had to abandon his plan of campaign and he broke off from the Helvetii, instead marching his army to the capital of the Aedui.[59]

Caesar's reliance on allies became a necessity, as rearward supply lines broke down as a result of the growing distance between Rome and the theatres of war. The apparatus required to defend extended supply lines from Italy or the strategic base – Narbonensis – was unsustainable. Requisition from allies and defeated foes was the only option. It was simple and cheap – and provided Caesar with new opportunities.

He was not the first Roman commander to requisition supplies, of course. During the first campaign of the Third Macedonian War (171–168 BC), for example, field marshals arranged for supplies from allies and from defeated peoples.[60] This was done despite tremendous preparations and the intention of having grain delivered from the Italian peninsula. During the Second Punic War, supply deliveries from Roman merchants and trading companies were common. In general, as the Roman Republic grew and the distances between Rome and the theatres of war became extended, it became increasingly difficult to organize the replenishing of supplies from traditional supply bases.

Caesar followed these precedents and relied on allies from the beginning of the Gallic campaigns. After the victory over the Helvetii, the Aedui continued to support the Romans. Moreover, the Ligones, a tribe settled just north of the Aedui, supplied corn during the march to Vesontio, where Caesar used the near-perfect geography to establish a garrison and to take advantage of the sufficient supplies on hand.[61] During the subsequent campaign against Ariovistus, the Aedui – assisted by the Sequani, Leuci and Lingones – took responsibility for supplying the Roman army.[62]

While receiving supplies from allies was not unprecedented, the Roman soldiers did not have complete confidence in the system. Some, in fact, channelled their fear of battle against the Germans into fear of lacking supplies: 'Those of them who desired to be thought less timid would declare that they were not afraid of the enemy, but feared the narrow defiles and the vast forests which lay between themselves and Ariovistus, or a possible failure of proper transport for the corn supply.'[63] Caesar convened a council and rebuked them – while underscoring that he took ultimate responsibility for the food supply:

> Those persons who ascribe their own cowardice to a pretended anxiety for the corn supply or to the defiles on the route are guilty of presumption, for they appear either to despair of the commander's doing his duty or to instruct him in it. These matters are my own concern; corn is being supplied by the Sequani, the Leuci, the Lingones and the corn crops in the fields are already ripe.[64]

Caesar's demand for grain from the Aedui had been a condition of the arrangement to undertake the initial campaign against the Helvetii. The same is true for the subsequent campaign against Ariovistus. Whether the allies were compensated for their deliveries is unknown, though in time compensation was common and distinguished whether a tribe had yielded and surrendered to the Romans or had fought them and were defeated.[65] Generally, after the initial defeat, payment was demanded and only after the grain was delivered did a new arrangement come into effect in which the Romans compensated the former foes for the grain. Even under these arrangements, however, the Romans insisted that the subjected peoples carry as much of the cost of the supplies as possible.

Caesar's frequent remarks on grain deliveries to Roman troops following surrender testify to their regularity. In 57 BC, the Remi, a Belgic tribe, immediately offered grain following their defeat.[66] The Remi subsequently replenished the Roman troops who were positioned further to the north.[67] During the second expedition to Britain, in 54 BC, Caesar ordered the first tribe he met, the Trinobantes, to supply grain. In short, it came to be understood that defeat meant far more than being vanquished in battle: defeat meant the tribe would carry the burden of supplying the Roman army.

The success of the system, moreover, meant that each victory increased the chances that the Roman army would be able to sustain itself so far from home.[68] As Caesar was able to secure an ever-wider position in Gaul, he did not need to press a single tribe into terms to resupply his army. Rather, Caesar was able to spread his demands among several tribes and establish a larger area from which to resupply his troops.

The delivery of grain followed a regular procedure that began after negotiations. Caesar concluded a treaty with the tribe's leaders or with their representatives. The treaty dictated the amount of grain to be delivered, as well as the time and location of the transfer.[69] The Gallic leaders were then responsible for their peoples' delivery. They were to bring it (in general, the Gauls used carts – 'carri' – and, when possible, riverboats[70]) to collection centres until it could be transported in larger quantities or in its entirety to the agreed upon location. The Gauls, moreover, were then responsible for the further transportation of the grain and its management.

During campaigns, the Gauls often followed the Roman army with grain. While campaigning against Ariovistus, the Gallic supply trains went back and forth between the Roman camps and their rear areas.[71] Shortly thereafter, in 57 BC, Caesar arranged the transports of the Remi and other tribes.[72] In Aquitaine, similarly, Crassus was dependent upon the Gallic transport to his rear.[73]

The allies were responsible for not only the management of the grain deliveries, but for security during transport as well. Safety was a challenge, as the many attacks on the Roman trains show, though there is a conspicuous absence of reports in Caesar's commentaries of the Romans providing any significant security during these operations. In fact, even during the difficult seventh year of the war, when virtually all of Gaul had risen up against the Romans, Caesar continued to have the Aedui, with their significant cavalry and considerable number of foot soldiers, provide security for the transport of grain, despite repeated experiences that proved they were not reliable.[74]

Allied contributions during the winter months provided special challenges and required specific procedures. Before Caesar released the tribes' leaders after the end of the year's campaigning, he held an autumn meeting in which the supply of the Roman troops during the winter was the most important topic. In 54 BC, for instance, Caesar mentioned the autumn conference that took place in Samarobriva (Amiens) before the dispersal of his legions to the winter camps.[75] The following year, the meeting was held in the Remi city of Durocortorum and Caesar noted that the winter's corn supply was arranged before he departed.[76] The challenge of delivering corn in winter, of course, was the condition of the roads and paths. Still, the allies were responsible for bring the grain to the Romans at the winter camps, a task made easier by the arrangement of tasking the tribes in the immediate vicinity with the deliveries.

Caesar continued to rely on his remaining allies during the final year of the Gallic campaigns, despite the widespread uprising.[77] He rushed to help the Boii against a threat from Vercingetorix, placing the responsibility for supplying his eight legions on the Aedui.[78] Yet after several defeats, Vercingetorix refused to engage in battle and opted instead for a scorched-earth policy that eliminated all possibilities of foraging. This strategy made Caesar all the more dependent on his remaining allies. The disadvantages of the system became ever clearer as the Roman army frequently entered into dangerous situations of dependency on the supply capabilities of foreign peoples. Time and again these partners proved to be unreliable.

In the winter of 52 BC, Caesar had strung together a series of victories against Vercingetorix at Vellaunodunum, Genabum and Noviodunum Biturigum. Vercingetorix, having lost the three battles, changed tactics. Instead of engaging the Romans, he adopted a Fabian strategy, preferring a war of attrition over direct battle. Like Caesar,

Vercingetorix wanted to deny the enemy grain supplies during this unproductive time of the year. The towns within reach of Caesar's forces were stripped bare and destroyed, moving all grain that could be transported and contaminating the rest. The scorched earth policy applied to the entire area except for Avaricorum, which Vercingetorix perceived to be impenetrable.

When Caesar arrived, Vercingetorix positioned his army 15 miles away, trapping Caesar's forces into an area that was unsuitable for forage. What made the situation dire was the inability – or unwillingness – of Caesar's remaining allies to supply his army with grain. The Aedui had quietly joined the Gallic rebellion and the Boii did not have even enough grain for themselves.[79] The Roman soldiers' diets became insufficient, even after substituting grain calories with those of meat.[80] The hunger became so acute that Caesar spoke personally to his troops, offering to lift the siege and withdraw if the scarcity of food was too great. In typical fashion, the Roman soldiers refused to entertain the thought, protesting that ending the siege would be a disgrace.

The Romans worked despite their hunger, building a ramp, complete with towers and a protective connecting wall. During the twenty-five days of construction, Vercingetorix's men repeatedly thwarted Roman attempts at forage, robbing the Romans of their remaining hope. Once the ramp was complete, however, fortune came and a storm struck, causing the Gallic sentries to abandon their posts and seek shelter. This allowed the Romans to move their construction into position without facing countermeasures.

Once the attack commenced, the *oppidum*'s walls fell quickly. The Romans surrounded the Gauls, who had mostly fled to the centre of the fortress. The Romans attacked, slaughtering all but a few hundred of the 40,000 Gauls.

To the victor goes the spoils. Caesar's soldiers remained at Avaricum until June, regaining their strength through rest and a steady diet of the Gauls' grain. Refortified, Caesar's army moved on and drew Vercingetorix into battle, a campaign that culminated in the siege of Alesia, the last major battle between the Gauls and the Romans.

In general, allied contributions of resources meant that the Caesarean army relied on the region more than on long supplies lines and trains coming from supply bases. But the local supply could not be overtaxed and abused. In fact, thrifty husbandry was to their advantage. As historian J.A. Lynn pointed out, 'they had to function like a well-evolved parasite and draw sustenance from the host, not kill it'.[81]

Requisitioning worked slightly differently during the Civil War, when ultimate victory was less about defeating the enemy than securing the support from the people who lived in the area of operations. Here, Caesar employed a different tactic, one that required the local populations to switch to his side.[82] When they switched allegiances, they were expected to provide grain. For example, in 49 BC the tribes in northern Spain allied with Caesar and he immediately demanded grain. Without apparent resistance, the Iberians rounded up their pack animals and brought their grain to the Roman camp.[83] Fortunately for the locals, individual campaigns during the Civil War did not last too long and the burden was generally not as great as it was in the Gallic War. Moreover, the people who lived in those theatres were familiar with the Roman way of war, which made it possible to organize the supply for the Caesarean army without much effort on the part of their leaders.

This is not to say that supply lines during the Civil War were non-existent. Spanish tribes initially supplied Caesar's camp near Ilerda,[84] though large transports from Gaul were delivered by Gallic allies and from Italy itself.[85] During the campaign in Greece, Caesar received supplies from Oricum.[86] Caesar's base near Dyrrachium was supplied from Epirus and Lissus.[87] In Africa, Caesar's allies did not carry out large transports, but they were required to provide the means of transport (carts, wagons, etc.) because Caesar was unable to bring them by ship.[88]

As in the Gallic War, battlefield success was the determining factor in Caesar's supply situation. During the first phase of the Spanish war, Caesar had difficulty winning over sufficient allies. Only after the naval victory at Massilia, when large numbers of people in northern Spain came over to his side, did his strategic position improve. With their cooperation, Caesar freed himself of his difficult supply situation.[89] Caesar not only ensured his supply with the help of allies, but Pompey's supply problems markedly deteriorated as he had previously relied on those same peoples. Pompey's inability to sustain his position was ultimately a decisive turning-point in the Spanish war. Similarly, the Pompeians were well prepared in Africa as they were able to control the land around them. During this time Caesar was only able to win a few cities to his side. After Caesar's victory over Scipio, however, many who had once been loyal to Pompey opened their doors to Caesar.

Thus Caesar was often able to requisition supplies during the Civil War. During the encirclement of Pompey, Epirus, Lissus and the Parthians delivered supplies to Caesar's troops.[90] After Caesar's defeat at Dyrrachium, he resupplied his troops with the help of the Thessalonican cities.[91]

Caesar reacted strongly when agreements were broken, whether in the Gallic War or the Civil War. The Aduatuci broke their agreement with Caesar[92] and Caesar took reprisals against those living in Uxellodunum[93] and against Gomphi.[94] This threat of punishment following broken agreements became a tool with which Caesar was able to hold onto occupied territories. Retribution, not surprisingly, was a reaction that Caesar carried over into his political behaviour, showing that he could be very hard on those who betrayed him.

The trend of relying on allies to supply Roman troops continued well into the Empire. Tacitus, expressing concern that the Empire was losing its independence, contrasted the contemporaneous situation by writing that 'in former times Italy conveyed supplies to distant theatres of operation for its legions'.[95] He was, of course, referring to the early Republic. He was silent on Caesar's heavy reliance on requisitioning during the late Republic, undoubtedly because Caesar's great success undermined Tacitus' point.

Pillage and Plunder

Whenever supply lines and requisitioning failed, there was always pillage and plunder, which consisted of the forced seizure of provisions and also, upon occasion, the destruction of property. Armies throughout history have pillaged, though the Roman version often had a discipline to it that was lacking elsewhere. The Roman army insisted that booty be turned in to military authorities, who redistributed it among the troops. Regulations prohibited unauthorized pillaging. Sextus Julius Frontinus, a first-century AD Roman senator, quoted Cato in saying that soldiers caught stealing could have their right hands cut off. (Stealing in a military camp, according to Polybius, resulted in a beating – *fustuarium* – at the hands of fellow soldiers.)

When pillage and plunder were employed, they were as often used as a weapon as they were a method of resupply. Caesar, in the campaign against Cassivellaunus, a chieftain who led a coalition of tribes in the defence of Britain, attempted to use his cavalry to 'plunder and devastate more freely' by releasing them throughout the fields along the Roman route of march.[96] Cassivellaunus's charioteers checked Caesar's cavalry and Caesar was limited to doing 'as much harm to the enemy in laying waste the fields and in conflagrations as the marching powers of the legionaries could accomplish'.[97] If provisions and supplies could not be obtained, Caesar was not going to allow the enemy to have them either.

Because of the strength of Caesar's supply lines, system of requisitioning and experienced foraging, his army was not dependent on plunder. However, it served several purposes. As mentioned, while obtaining provisions was a benefit, at least equally important was the destruction of the enemy's supplies. The benefits of striking terror into the enemy – and sometimes wavering allies or ambivalent neutrals – was also well known. Pillaging, finally, was also used to raise the spirits of demoralized troops.

Yet Caesar knew it was often preferable to maintain good relations with a local population, so the proscription against stealing from inhabitants while on the march was often strictly enforced. When Caesar arrived in Africa in 47 BC, he forbade looting in an attempt to win the sympathy of the locals.[98] The attempt was ultimately unsuccessful, but at least the effort showed Roman restraint. Not surprisingly, control broke down considerably during times of civil war or under commanders with lax discipline.[99] When legionaries stole and pillaged individually, Caesar criticized them and tried to restore order.[100]

A common result of plundering was the depletion of resources in the countryside. That was the aim if an army was simply passing through, but it needed to be avoided if the army was dependent upon the resources. Regardless, the loss of seed corn and the loss of animal labour power could cause more damage than simply the loss of the plundered or foraged goods, since it depleted the means of future production.[101] Caesar often forbade the devastation of the countryside, in part because it endangered the future food supply.[102]

Personal Acquisition and Private Trade

The most common ancillary method of supply was the personal purchase of desired food items through local vendors. Caesar's army was accompanied by sutlers, individuals who followed an army on the march, often maintaining a store near the camp to sell provisions to the soldiers. Sutlers did not provide bulk food like grain, but were instead used as a source from which to purchase luxury or gourmet items to vary their diet. Such items included oil, vinegar, fish sauce and spices.[103] Local merchants could have sold what they obtained locally – local farmers or merchants often used sutlers as middlemen to provide goods to armies – or they could have imported the goods from elsewhere. Through the examination of privately sold amphorae containing plants and plant-food products there is significant evidence to demonstrate that long-distance trading to support culinary desires was common.[104] Regardless, private trade existed on every possible level, a mechanism that has supplied food to armies throughout history.

The number of sutlers accompanying an army depended almost entirely on the region in which the campaign took place. When Caesar's army fought in wealthy regions, which was more often than not around the Mediterranean, sutlers were bound to follow – especially if Caesar's troops were successful and the individual soldiers had acquired sufficient booty with which to trade. In these situations, sutlers often had their own lengthy train of pack animals to carry supplies, in addition to all of the various trains of the army. They set up their own tents outside the army camp. It is unclear to what extent they could expect protection in hostile territories. In poorer regions, such as much of Gaul, it was hardly worth the sutlers' effort to accompany the army.

Caesar tolerated the presence of sutlers and petty traders. In fact, they provided a service. Officers – often hypocritically – discouraged the accumulation of booty among the soldiers and thus the sutlers and traders provided an opportunity to unload unwanted goods in exchange for consumable foodstuffs.[105] However, even if officers encouraged the presence of private trade, it was never a centralized structure, it did not provide a significant amount of supplies and it was never depended upon. It was, rather, an additional, perhaps gratuitous, source of food. It provided a welcome change of flavour and, almost certainly, nutritional diversity. Vegetables and fruit, which never travelled well over long distances and did not store well, were undoubtedly most frequently available through private trade with locals (through sutlers), even if the demand for such products was generally low.

Another common practice was to hunt local game while off duty. By doing so a soldier might introduce fresh meat into his diet; wild birds, venison and wild boar were all hunted when time permitted.[106] And, finally, still another way for a soldier to add to his cuisine was to make requests to relatives. There is significant evidence found in letters between soldiers and relatives requesting all manner of goods: wine, oils, bread, fish, fruit (olives, apples, coconuts, etc.), vegetables (asparagus, beans, cabbage, etc.), salt and mustard, to name a few.[107] This, of course, occurred almost exclusively while legions were garrisoned in the Republic itself or in a semi-permanent base.

Together, the methods to provide foodstuffs combined to create a complex system that helped the Caesarean army avoid starvation. While foraging, plunder and private trade generally supplemented requisition and the supply lines, they also served as emergency backup measures if the army became disconnected from its operational bases. Requisitioning was the most important element of Caesar's supply system and, like foraging, was used to support operations where supply lines were either strained or compromised. Just as with foraging, a large army or a prolonged stay could exhaust local resources. Furthermore, requisitioning incurred a certain political cost as local inhabitants lost crops and livestock to military needs.

Honey Pine Nut Custard

This custard recipe is wholesome, nourishing and filling. Apicius suggested sprinkling pepper on top of honey custard before serving. The basic recipe for honey custard has remained the same for a millennium, however custard has been a main dish, a food to build strength in the sickly and a pie filling. The concept of a formal dessert course is a fairly modern idea. This recipe uses caramelized pine nuts and makes the perfect personal sized dessert.

Ingredients:
350ml/14 fl oz honey, divided into two containers, one with 250ml/10 fl oz and the other with 100ml/4 fl oz
30g/1 cup pine nuts
600ml/3 cups milk
200ml/1 cup cream
4 large eggs
4 egg yolks
bread or cake

Directions:
Place a kettle of water over medium heat. Preheat the oven to 160°C/325°F/Gas 3.

Place 250ml/10 fl oz of honey in a pan and cook over medium to high heat until reduced a bit and amber coloured. Toss in the pine nuts and stir until caramelized.

Coat the bottom and sides of 8 small ramekins with the caramel, dividing pine nuts evenly among the cups and let cool. Place cups in a roasting pan.

Heat milk and cream together until warm. Do not allow to boil. In a bowl, whisk large eggs, egg yolks and remaining 100ml/4 fl oz honey together. Continue to whisk while slowly pouring in cream and milk. When blended, divide mixture among prepared ramekins.

Pour hot water from kettle into the roasting pan, to come halfway up the sides of the ramekins. Bake until barely set, about 30 minutes, until the centres are just firm but still jiggle a bit. Remove from roasting pan and chill.

Cut slices of bread or cake approximately ½ in thick. With a biscuit cutter, cut a circle the same size as the ramekin. To serve, loosen the edge of the custard and invert onto the break or cake round, onto a plate.

Makes 8 servings.

Chapter 6

Logistics and Strategy

The principle point in war is to secure plenty of
provisions and to destroy the enemy by famine.
Vegetius, *Epitome of Military Science*

Military commanders value both flexibility of movement and the security of their forces. The problem, of course, is that these two conditions are often contradictory. In ancient warfare, allowing armies to live off the land often increased flexibility. At times, this required straightforward plundering. Independence from supply lines and bases allowed armies to go where the commanders wanted them to go. Living off the land, however, dramatically decreased the security of the forces. Which condition – flexibility or security – was most valued often depended on the individual commander and the situation, though military leaders always considered the relationship between logistics and strategy.

Ancient military thinking took it for granted that depriving your adversary of sustenance was a legitimate part of warfare. 'Famine makes a greater havoc in an army than the enemy and is more terrible than the sword', Vegetius wrote in *On Roman Military Matters*,[1] affirming that the commander must give due diligence to logistical planning before a campaign. Obviously, this included accounting for the number of troops he had and the logistical needs of those troops. To meet these needs, he had to arrange for grain from the provinces and allies in a timely manner – before the commencement of the campaign – so that they could gather and provide the army its requirements. It was also necessary to ensure the collection of provisions through requisition from defeated foes and foraging. If this was achieved, then 'the troops should never want wood and forage in winter or water in summer. They should have corn, wine, vinegar and even salt, in plenty at all times.'[2]

Julius Caesar's great success depended in part on his ability to link food supply logistics to strategy. Not only were his strategic – and sometimes tactical – decisions informed by aspects of the food supply, but he knew that food (or lack thereof) could be as potent a weapon as the sword. Sextus Julius Frontinus, a Roman senator writing in the late first century AD, quoted Caesar on the use of logistics in military strategy: 'I follow the same policy toward the enemy as did many doctors when dealing with physical ailments, namely, that of conquering the foe by hunger rather than by steel.'[3] Caesar was not alone among Roman military leaders who recognized that food supply could be used as a weapon, but he may have been the Republic's foremost practitioner of such strategy and tactics. Questions of when and where Caesar's army fought were often dependent on whether the army could be properly supplied. The Dyrrachium campaign, for example, showed how Caesar went on the offensive earlier than planned because Pompey's greater food supply would have given him a distinct advantage if Caesar had delayed.[4]

Food supply strategy was also used against Caesar. Vercingetorix understood Caesar's predicament – both geographical obstacles and distance cut Caesar off from supplies from the Mediterranean – and designed his strategy directly toward taking out Caesar's food supply.

During the Civil War, particularly throughout 49 and 48 BC, Caesar had to act more swiftly than he otherwise would have, which often left him with inadequate preparation of his food supply. While Caesar's speed often surprised his adversaries, it also left him vulnerable. More often than not, however, Caesar's swiftness caught his opponents off guard and was the singular element of his strategy that determined his final victory.

The Role of Supply in the Gallic War

Gaul was almost as densely populated as much of Italy on the eve of Caesar's campaigns. The region was saturated with *oppida*, fortified settlements with economic activity and some form of political centralization. Throughout Gaul, agrarian activity flourished and animal husbandry was common. Caesar mentioned twenty-eight *oppida* of various sizes.[5] Trade flourished among them but there was also regular import and export activity. To find evidence of the well-developed supply planning of the Gauls, one need read no further than the opening of the first book of *De Bello Gallico*, in which Caesar mentions how the Helvetii prepared for their exodus over a period of two years.[6] In short, the sum of the Gallic supply methods suggests that the necessary elements to supply the Gallic armies existed in Gaul, including pathways and means of transport.[7]

Yet all of these existing supply conditions raises a question. If the Gauls possessed all of the necessary components of a sufficient supply system and if the playing field was more or less level in terms of quantity of supply and the potential to deliver rations to their fighting men, then why were the Romans vastly superior when it came to supplying their forces? The answer is found in the comparative military cultures, especially in the higher value the Romans placed on supply.

The Roman army was institutionalized, regulated and professional; it was led by experienced field commanders; tactics and strategy followed principles of Roman military experience; the culture of the Roman army was defined by organization, discipline and experienced leadership. The Gauls, in contrast, simply had not reached this level of military development. Roman superiority was not a result of material superiority, nor better weapons technology, of which the Romans had at best a slight advantage. Rather, the Romans knew how to wage war – and they understood the importance of supply in that endeavour.

The Gauls, Caesar's writings make clear, were well-stocked and prepared at the beginning of a battle.[8] However, their tactics were less cautious and there is little evidence of lengthy planning, especially in terms of their supply needs.[9] Instead, the Gauls sought to force the enemy into battle as quickly as possible in order to push them back in a ferocious initial contact. Caesar recognized this tactic in the early campaigns of the Helvetii,[10] the Germani[11] and the Nervii.[12] In turn, because the Gauls did not themselves pay significant attention to their own supply needs, they also did not initially recognize the important role of supply in Roman fighting capability.

Only in time, after observing Roman supply methods, did they concentrate their attacks on that aspect of the Roman war machine. The Sotiates had fought the Romans in several battles prior to their attack on Publius Crassus in Aquitania in 56 BC. While they had scored victories, none were lasting. When they attacked Crassus in Aquitania, however, they did so without haste and they focused their attack on the Romans' supplies rather than the army itself.[13] This shows the tribe's ability to learn after just a few battles with their Roman enemy.

In contrast, the Britons refrained from thoughtless actions from the start, even though they had had no contact with the Roman army. At the beginning of the first invasion of Britain, they witnessed the extensive Roman war techniques. When a significant portion of Caesar's fleet was destroyed in a storm, the Britons cut off the remaining Roman legion in order to prevent it from being resupplied. Their hope was to prolong the campaign into the winter, knowing that the Romans did not have sufficient resources to maintain their forces on the island.[14] The Britons also ambushed the VII Legion while it foraged for corn. The legion would have been annihilated were it not for a speedy response by the remaining Roman troops, who were able to support them and bring them safely back to the camp.[15]

The backbone of the Britons' defensive campaign, in fact, was the attempt to prevent the Romans from supplying their army. The isolation of the Roman camp and the inability to resupply it promised that the Romans would be pulled into a longer campaign that would consistently weaken then, which the Britons would exploit and eventually then destroy.

Despite the value that Caesar placed on provisioning his troops, one is struck again and again by the difficulties that beset his men while he campaigned in Gaul. In the campaign against the Helvetii, supply difficulties hindered the Romans.[16] In the campaign against Ariovistus, supply lines repeatedly broke down.[17] Shortages plagued the winter camps of 54–53 BC. Deficiencies of provisioning in the years 53 to 51 BC made the ability to conduct war difficult, as the battles at Avaricum and Alesia made clear.[18] Simply put, despite the importance Caesar gave to provisioning, he often had difficulties providing for his troops while he was in Gaul and this had a negative impact on his success on the battlefield.

The Role of Supply in the Civil War

The initial situation in the Civil War was considerably different than it had been in the Gallic War. Caesar's opponents had the same military tradition and a similar military organization. Moreover, the importance placed on supply was equal on both sides. Far more than in Gaul, tactical and strategic decisions – on both sides – revolved around protecting their food supplies while attacking those of their enemies.

Lucius Afranius and Marcus Petreius were well-prepared opponents of Caesar's in Spain. They encamped their five legions at Ilerda, a location chosen largely because of its strategic position.[19] They had stockpiled large quantities of grain and animal feed in the city and had reserves in the surrounding area. More significantly, because the area that Caesar would operate had been plundered, conditions for supplying his troops in the area were poor.[20] His inability to capture Massilia, moreover, forced Caesar to organize supply trains from Gaul and Italy, lengthy routes that were exposed to enemy attack and were at the mercy of unpredictable weather.[21]

The Pompeians thwarted Caesar's attempts to free himself of the poor supply situation. His foraging troops were captured, hostile forces prevented him from building bridges, his trains were redirected into the mountains and Afranius' troops watched the routes leading to Caesar's position.[22] The situation was dire and Caesar felt as though he were being besieged. Grain prices from his few Spanish allies rose dramatically and Caesar's troops were forced to rely on meat for their strength and calorific intake.[23] The Roman world expected the certain defeat of Julius Caesar.[24]

Three events saved Caesar in Spain. First, he was finally able to build a bridge, 33km north of his camp. The significance of this is that the bridge enabled him to get supply trains to his camp.[25] Second, at the same time the bridge was built, news of the Caesarean naval victory at Massilia arrived.[26] Third and most significantly, the Spanish tribes, upon hearing of the sea battle, switched allegiance and came to Caesar's side. This was the decisive turning point in the campaign. The realignment completely turned the situation for Caesar because he could now supply his troops and Pompey's supply lines were compromised.[27]

Afranius and Petreius abandoned their now vulnerable position at Ilerda and marched to an area populated by allies, extending the war into the winter.[28] Caesar, who had calculated a quick end to the war, went in pursuit, despite difficult river crossings and hostile territory. Although he succeeded in pinning the Pompeians in the mountains,[29] he consistently refused to engage in battle. After four days without fodder and with serious shortages of water, wood and grain, the Pompeians surrendered.[30]

Looked at as a whole, the Spanish campaign proceeded in three phases. After the strategic offensive, Caesar, because of his limited preparation, was forced into an indecisive, desperate, tactically static warfare against an opponent who was defensively arranged because of his strategic position and well-stocked stores. Caesar's tactical actions were aimed against the Pompeian supply lines in the hope of dislodging them from their position. The supply situation influenced the Pompeian strategy as well as Caesar's tactical moves during the first phase of the campaign.

In the following two phases, replenishment of supplies determined the course of the war. The disruption of Caesar's supply lines constricted his troops in operational planning. His already insufficient base became so constricted that he could no longer feed his army. It must be emphasized that poor provisioning was the primary cause of Caesar's desperate situation at Ilerda. This situation was itself the result of other factors, including the long, insecure supply lines, the behaviour of the Spanish tribes and the unclear situation at Massilia. General strategic, operational and tactical factors were interdependent on Caesar's leadership style and his decisions regarding provisioning. The Pompeians had every reason to expect an easy victory over an isolated, weakened opponent.

In this situation, the course of events and Caesar's ultimate victory had little to do with his military actions. Rebuilding the bridge alone was insufficient to restore his fortunes. The new bridge and the slight improvement of Caesar's position did little to influence the behaviour of the Spanish tribes. Rather, it was the victory at Massilia, which led the Spanish tribes to switch sides, that dramatically improved Caesar's general situation. With the realignment of allies, the Pompeian position became untenable. Thereafter, Caesar could play out his tactical skill while pursuing his retreating opponent and prevent his enemy from replenishing his supplies. His ultimate victory came without engaging the enemy in battle.

During the campaign in Africa, Caesar was in a similarly disadvantaged position. While the Pompeians could remain in a defensive position and make decisions free of concerns about provisions, Caesar's actions were determined by his state of supply. Again, he made up for insufficient preparation with surprise and speed. Caesar had enormous deficiencies, especially of fodder, during the entire campaign. He had to increase his provisions from the surrounding territory and set about doing so through foraging, requisition and the storming of enemy supply bases – methods to which his soldiers were by now well accustomed. During the entire African campaign, however, Caesar maintained strong connections between his camp and the coast. This helped him out of threatening situations such as the encirclement at Ruspina.

One of the most remarkable episodes related to supply – or more accurately, lack thereof – occurred at Dyrrachium in 48 BC Caesar's troops had laid siege to Pompey's well-fortified and well-provisioned army despite being desperately short of food. Given the option to break the siege in order to resupply, Caesar's men indicated that they would rather eat tree bark than do so, assuring Caesar that the prospect of the coming harvest was sufficient to carry them through the siege.[31] In the meantime, they made bread from ground-up roots – but rather than eating it, they threw it into Pompey's camp to demoralize his soldiers.[32] The message was clear. The food shortage would not cause Caesar's legions to abandon the siege.

During the Civil War, the impression that Caesar struggled to provision his troops is even stronger than it had been in Gaul. The regions in which he fought had often been fully plundered and he fought against an opponent with equal military strength, an opponent who was well prepared and who often had local allies on his side. The Spanish campaign of 49 BC and the campaigns against Pompey and Scipio were characterized by Caesar struggling to secure his supplies. The impression that Caesar's soldiers lived hand-to-mouth is inescapable when one thinks of Ilerda, Dyrrachium and Ruspina. That Caesar left everything behind when he departed for Greece and for Africa, that he made virtually no preparations and that he was well aware of the risks involved with the supply line made the difficulties in supplying his troops inevitable as soon as the first setbacks of the war came. While the supply problems in the Gallic War had been a result of the geographic circumstances, in the Civil War, Caesar expected supply problems, he was willing to accept the risks and he was confident he would overcome them.

If anything, we are left with a contradiction: on the one hand, Caesar appreciated the importance of provisioning and knew it to be vital to his success. On the other, he conducted the war, especially during the Civil War, in such a way that was almost to guarantee that supply difficulties would arise. The way out of this contradiction is to appreciate the way in which Caesar led on the battlefield. Caesar sought the tactical advantage and this was gained through speed; provisioning his troops cost precious time. Speed, even with tremendous costs, was the preeminent characteristic of his campaigns.

Caesar's style of leadership can be seen in a speech, recorded by Appian, that Caesar gave to his soldiers on the eve of sailing to Greece:

> Fellow soldiers – you who are joined with me in the greatest of undertakings – neither the winter weather, nor the delay of our comrades, nor the want of suitable preparation shall check my onset. I consider rapidity of movement the best substitute for all these things. I think that we who are first at the rendezvous should leave behind us here our servants, our pack-animals and all our apparatus in order that ships which are here may hold us and that we should embark alone and cross over at once without the enemy's knowledge. Let us oppose our good fortune to the winter weather, our courage to the smallness of our numbers and to our want of supplies the abundance of the enemy, which will be ours to take as soon as we touch the land, if we realize that unless we conquer nothing is our own. Let us go then and possess ourselves of their

servants, their apparatus, their provisions, while they are spending the winter under cover. Let us go while Pompey thinks that I am spending my time in winter quarters also, or in processions and sacrifices appertaining to my consulship. It is needless to tell you that the most potent thing in war is unexpectedness.[33]

The speech includes all of the points of Caesar's leadership in war. Supply preparation was worth risking; the speed of their arrival would surprise the defensively-positioned opponent; in the case of victory, the preparations of the enemy – their supplies – would then help the victorious attackers.

The contradiction between Caesar's comment about the importance of supply and his actual conduct can in part be explained by his development as a field commander. He had confidence that his experienced legions would overcome shortages, whether through reconnected supply lines, requisition, forage or plunder. More important, though, was his style of leadership. Caesar was committed to taking the offensive, whether as a general strategy or as part of his operational and tactical decision-making. He was often willing to take tremendous risks, courting difficulties regarding supplies. Where preparation and organization were lacking, he made up for in improvisation and quick responses to new situations.

Moreover, Caesar's army learned how to improvise during the Gallic War and applied those lessons to the Civil War. The experience and methods they learned in Gaul – foraging, requisitioning, replacing usual foods with alternatives – were passed on to new legions and new recruits. At Dyrrachium, they made flour out of roots, which they mixed with milk to ameliorate the bitter taste. They were able to turn it into *puls* and even baked bread.[34] In Ruspina, they prepared seaweed with fresh water to feed their horses. These innovations increasingly gave Caesar more flexibility and Caesar even heaped praise on his soldiers and cavalry for their knowledge and experience.[35]

Attacking Food Supplies

One of the most effective strategies related to food supplies was blockade. Roman commanders cut off or blocked the enemy's supplies whenever possible, either by preventing the enemy from accessing overland or waterborne supplies or by making foraging and requisition difficult. Even preventing *pabulatio*, the forage for fodder, was highly effective. The rapid starvation of animals crippled the enemy's ability to move and Caesar indicated that such blockades were a common practice.[36]

An enemy's water supply was, of course, especially important – and therefore an attractive target. Cutting off the water supply was a more effective logistical weapon than blocking the food supply, at least on a tactical level. Both men and animals can survive much longer without food than they can without water. Caesar's victory during the Ilerda campaign in 49 BC was at least in part a result of his ability to cut off the enemy's water supply.[37] Conversely, Caesar indicated that enemy forces at times interfered with troops gathering water outside of his army's camps.

The Gallic tribes eventually came to understand the effectiveness of blocking and towards the end of the conflict it became common practice for the Gauls to cut off Roman access to their supplies. At the very least, blocking was less daunting than trying to defeat the Roman army in battle. In *De Bello Gallico* Caesar repeatedly mentions various tribes – the Helvetii, Suebi, Britons – as well as the coalition led by Vercingetorix as trying to cut off his army from their supplies.[38] In particular, Vercingetorix understood the Roman dependency on forage in 52 BC He instructed his commanders to consider long-term goals rather than short-term victories from direct battle. As Caesar recounted it:

> [Vercingetorix] did not purpose to try his fortune or fight a pitched battle; but, as he had an abundance of horsemen, it was easy enough to prevent the Romans from getting corn and forage. Only, the Gauls must consent to destroy with their own hands their corn-supplies and burn their buildings, seeing that by such loss of property they were acquiring dominion and liberty for all time.[39]

Whether conducted by the Caesarean army or by its enemies, the goal was always the same: restricting supply, whether at the strategic or tactical level. This could prevent unwanted battles with the enemy or, in extreme situations, lead to the enemy's surrender.

Pillaging, of course, was also a weapon against the enemy's supplies in so far as the goal was often to destroy the enemy's supplies as much as it was to gain foodstuffs for the pillagers. Together with attacking supply lines and even trying to capture strategic bases, pillaging was part of a strategy that targeted logistics.

The food supply during military operations was often inadequate, a condition that by no means was limited to the Romans and antiquity. But the cause of this inadequacy was rarely organization or the ability to transport supplies from point A to point B, even if they were far from each other. Rather, the cause of the inadequacy was more often either the behaviour of the commanders, who often pushed aggressively to gain advantage, or the enemy's effectiveness at disrupting well-planned resupply procedures. Caesar was no exception. He prioritized speed and surprise over stability and security and left his army open to enemy blocking of the food supply. Had he prioritized safety of the food supply, he would have compromised his offensive capability leading to a static condition of warfare. And for Caesar, if you weren't attacking, you were vulnerable.

During the Civil War, food supply was a consideration in the strategies of both Caesar and Pompey. After Caesar's surprise landing in Epirus in 48 BC, he positioned his army between Pompey's army and its principal magazine in Dyrrachium, cutting his enemy off from his supplies. However, this left Caesar in a poor position. He seemed to have not considered Pompey's flexibility on the Adriatic coast. Pompey had the advantage of naval superiority and was able to obtain provisions from overseas. Caesar's army, meanwhile, had no secure food supply. Pompey rightfully avoided battle with Caesar, realizing that time would weaken Caesar's army.

Realizing Pompey was waiting him out, Caesar drove inland, away from the enemy. It was less a retreat than a strategic change to a more conducive position. The idea was twofold: to search for supplies in areas in which Pompey's army had not yet exploited and to draw Pompey away from his well-supplied position on the coast. Caesar wrote that his plan was 'to be always on the march, with the view of getting his supplies more conveniently by moving camp and visiting various places'.[40] Caesar's actions must have weakened Pompey's resolve to wait out Caesar, especially because his officers and members of the Senate pressured him to engage. The result, the Battle of Pharsalus, was decisive, a victory for Caesar which changed the course of the war.

The siege, finally, was a technique used in antiquity to capture the food supplies defended behind a town's walls. Yet they were extremely difficult military undertakings. Locals naturally brought everything they could carry from the surrounding areas inside the walls, depriving the besieging army of necessary supplies. By definition, sieges – as opposed to storming the walled town – were an attempt to starve out those inside. Yet it was just as likely that the besieging army, relying on the depleted surrounding countryside, suffered the same state of starvation.

Defending Food Supplies

Roman military manuals such as *De Re Militari* emphasized the need to protect supply lines from enemy attack.[41] All elements of the supply chain – operational bases, tactical bases, supply lines – were vital to the

110

success of the entire campaign. Of course, the loss of an operational base would be an unmitigated disaster, disrupting supply lines going back to the source of supply and leaving an entire army vulnerable for the duration in the field of operations.

We have seen how the Romans relied heavily on seaborne transport. It provided a quick and efficient link between the sources of supply and the operational bases. But water transport was not invulnerable to attack. During the Alexandrian campaign in 48–47 BC, the Egyptians cut off Caesar's seaborne supply line by stationing ships in the Nile delta.[42] Caesar survived only by requesting the aid of his ally Mithridates of Pergamum, who marched his army from Asia Minor to join up with Caesar's. Together, the 20,000-strong army defeated the Egyptians at the Battle of the Nile in February 47 BC.

Overland supply routes were more frequently vulnerable. The enemy did not need to mount as sophisticated an attack to block the transport. The threat of ambush was constant and Caesar assigned significant numbers of troops to protect convoys. Moreover, he ensured that the area through which the supply lines ran, from the operational base to the army, was sufficiently pacified. Whenever army trains and troop trains were on the move, the supplies were placed within a protective screen of troops, a practice advocated in Roman military manuals. Tacitus himself indicated that 'a lengthy baggage train is easy to ambush and awkward to defend'.[43] Polybius also warned of the vulnerability of trains.[44] Although both wrote after Caesar's time, it was not a lesson Caesar needed to learn.

Once the supplies arrived at the tactical base, fortifications were necessary against the expected attacks. The threat of attack against supplies was among the reasons for the development of the marching camp, which often acted as the tactical base. Protecting the food supply was as important as protecting the men. The very site of the camp, of course, was chosen with defence in mind. The location could not stretch the supply lines too thin and there had to be a safe area to forage for fodder, water and firewood. Water carriers were at most risk, though foragers for fodder and firewood were not left unmolested. Part of Caesar's defensive strategy for protecting this aspect of the food supply was to send out foraging parties at different times and along different routes, with guards and they never strayed far from camp.[45]

Sausages with Fried Cardoons served with Endive Salad

Fried cardoons are a dish most common to Southern Italy, Spain and parts of France. Cardoons resemble celery and are an edible thistle. Commercially-grown stalks can grow to be several feet long and quite thick. Wild cardoons are found in temperate climates and tend to have smaller, tenderer stalks. They have a rich flavour, similar to an artichoke. For those seeking garden-fresh vegetables, cardoon seeds are available online. They are perennials and grow best in full sun, but can tolerate some shade. Fresh cardoons can last up to one week in the refrigerator.

Ingredients:
680g / 1.5lb sausages of your choice
1,135g / 2.5lb cardoons
Juice of 3 lemons
350g / 1.5 cups flour
Vegetable oil for frying
2 Tbsp olive oil
Salt and pepper to taste

Directions:
Wash cardoons; remove and discard outer stalks. Trim thorns and stringy fibres from each stalk with a knife or peeler (like peeling the strings from a stalk of celery). Cut cardoons into 5cm / 2in pieces. Place in a pot of salted water with lemon juice.

Bring to a simmer over medium-high heat and cook until cardoons are tender, about 30 minutes. Drain, cool and dry with paper towels.

While cardoons are cooling, sauté sausage in 1 to 2 Tbsps. of olive oil for about 15 minutes until completely cooked. Place flour in a bowl and season with salt and pepper to taste. Add cardoons and toss until coated in flour mixture.

Heat 3cm / 1in of oil in a large skillet over medium-high heat.

Drop the floured cardoons into the hot oil. Fry in batches until golden, drain on paper towels, salt while still warm.

Makes 4 servings.

Endive Salad

Ingredients:
(All quantities are to taste.)
Endive
Lemon juice
Olive oil
Salt and pepper

Directions:
Wash and drain endive.

Drizzle dry endive with lemon juice, olive oil, salt and pepper to taste.

Chapter 7

A Modern North African Campaign

Commanders must base all their concepts of operation
on what they know they can do logistically.

Former United States Marine Corps
Commandant Alfred M. Gray, Jr.

Caesar's Civil War lasted from 49–45 BC and its component actions occurred across the continents of Europe, Asia and Africa. The campaigns specific to Africa occurred from 48–47 BC in Egypt and in 46 BC in modern-day Tunisia. Interestingly, almost exactly 2,000 years later, those same locations would feel not the footsteps of Rome's heavy legions, but the rumble of the mechanized forces fielded by the belligerents of the Second World War. From Tunisia to Egypt, between 1940 and 1943, the Axis and Allies fought elastic campaigns as Germany and Italy tried to wrest control of North Africa from the British. In November 1942, a second front was opened against the Vichy French as Operation Torch kicked off with Allied landings in Morocco and Algeria. The combined forces of the Axis and Allies settled the question of dominance in North African on 13 May 1943 as the Axis forces collapsed after being out-numbered, out-manoeuvred and ultimately out-supplied.

Despite the 2,000-year difference, the logistical infrastructure – sources of supply, operational bases, tactical bases, supply lines and trains – were comparable, suggesting that Julius Caesar had tapped into a timeless framework in which to wage war. Moreover, the questions that have guided this book – how did commanders feed an army so far from home, what did the soldiers eat and drink, how much did the individual soldier carry, what role did requisitioning and the local economy play, how were food supply and strategy linked – are just as pertinent when discussing the twentieth century as they are regarding antiquity.

The Allied North African campaign of the Second World War was a battle of logistical attrition. In desert terrain and mountain passes that were so inhospitable that nearly every logistical need would have to be shipped or flown into theatre, two of the most technologically-advanced forces of their day duelled it out, relying on the thinnest of logistical tethers. As road and rail infrastructure was not particularly robust and was generally limited to lines that serviced the coast, the control of ports would provide the logistical hubs that enabled the longitudinal traversing of mechanized and motorized forces vying for control of North Africa. This challenge overlaid a deficit in newly-minted operational planners lacking an understanding of the operational art. Being one of the first joint campaigns of significant magnitude, Allied planners embarked on a trying campaign of discovery learning.

This chapter focuses on the Allied side of logistical considerations; comparative anecdotes to Axis logistical consideration, however, will be made. Both the Axis and Allied forces contended with similar logistical concerns, be they inhospitable terrain, a dearth of logistical infrastructure and lines of communication that were both lengthy and vulnerable. More specifically, this chapter will discuss the nature of the operating environment, a brief diagram of logistical infrastructure from the point of origin to the forward edge of troops, how logistics impacted the individual soldier in terms of loads carried and food eaten, fuel demands and its logistical impacts on mechanized warfare, the ability to 'live off the land' by using local resources and ultimately, how logistical concerns affected the strategies employed by the ground commander.

While the geography of North Africa was relatively unchanged since Caesar's Civil War, the transportation network of the region had developed – but only slightly. If one were to bifurcate the North African theatre in the vicinity of the Tunisian Dorsal off of the Aurés Mountains, two distinct topographies, both equally inhospitable, would be readily apparent. To the east, one finds the Western Desert stretching from Libya to Egypt. As in Caesar's time, this zone is an area of no vegetation and virtually no water. The single most significant piece of transportation infrastructure in the mid-twentieth century was a road that followed the Mediterranean coast, undoubtedly following a merchant route that had existed for millennia. Beyond this road, unimproved desert tracks crisscrossed the landscape. The coast consists of a narrow sandy strip that varies in width from 12 to 38 miles, but its relative flatness expands inland as it approaches the Egyptian border. Moving further inland, the steeply rising Libyan Plateau, formed of limestone and thinly covered with sand, defined the region. Barring the requirement to use one of the passes to access the plateau, the area consists of flat to undulating barren plains of which mechanized tacticians dream.[1]

To the west from the Tunisian Dorsal through Algeria and terminating in Morocco, one finds terrain dominated by the varying ranges of the Atlas Mountains that touch the coast and stretch across the hinterland. Undulating steppe-like plains connect the area between the various Atlas ranges. While the infrastructure was slightly better than the Western Desert, it too would frustrate military logisticians. The limited road network that did exist either provided access to the coast from a few inland population centres, or traversed the Mediterranean coast from east to west along passes found on the coastal side of the Rif, Middle Atlas and Tell Atlas mountains. The primary infrastructural difference existing in the eastern zone was some additional road and rail routes that supported either east-west traversing or coastal access routes from points inland. Aside from the more coastal road there were a few, roughly parallel, inland routes that traversed the southern side of the Middle and Tell Atlas ranges that buttressed the coast. Additionally, a standard-gauge railway line stretched east to west and connected the ports from Morocco to Tunisia. This was fed by several 1m, narrow-gauge lines that connected lesser ports or inland centres to the main line and was the only gauge of track found throughout northern Tunisia.[2]

So how then did the Allies supply a seesaw campaign against the Axis for nearly three years? The short answer is that it was a campaign of ports from which the belligerents attached elastic logistical lifelines that were fed by some of the longest shipping routes seen in the war. While some limited support was flown into theatre, the vast majority was moved via sealift along sea lines of communication to ports and then via ground lines of communication, all the while running reciprocal gauntlets of enemy interdiction, be it under the water, in the air above, or along the surface.

Allied Supply Lines

Generally, both the Axis and Allies fed, supplied and reinforced their armies via sea lines that originated from their home territories; the exception being that some supply that made its way to the Commonwealth Western Desert Force (eventually to become the British Eighth Army) fighting in Egypt originated from the Middle

116

East. These supply lines from distant continents were part of a complex multi-tiered logistical system that started with sources of supply: home country supply depots, moved to ports of embarkation, loaded onto shipping assets, offloaded to supply dumps collocated with the ports of debarkation, then pushed onward to operational bases and ultimately to forward staging points to be distributed to the consuming units. In theory, this supply system was comparable to the Roman system.

While British planners had some level of experience in supplying their forces, American planners for Operation Torch went through a difficult process of discovery learned as they came to grips with the operational level of war. At the strategic level, the American War Department planners could produce and stage what they needed to support the grand war effort and at the tactical level, the various task force commanders rehearsed and understood supply. The challenge rested with marrying the two together. Theatre command and control, as it related to supplying the force, was neither trained for, nor experienced in, logistics. There was no clearly understood system for moving supply from the strategic to the tactical level.[3] In this regard, Caesar had an advantage of which Allied commanders could only dream: knowledge and experience gained from centuries of Roman warfare.

Before the outbreak of hostilities that brought America into the war, the War Department exercised centralized control between the zone of interior supply depots and the port of embarkation commander who served as a simple conduit to the theatre commander. After December 1941, this changed and the War Department relinquished significant control to the port of embarkation commander who now regulated the flow of supply requisitions. The system was used to support Operation Bolero, a plan that called for a massive build-up of American forces in the United Kingdom to support a forcible entry into the European mainland by crossing the English Channel. Later it was adjusted to support the build-up of US Army Air Forces in the United Kingdom. In the new system, the theatre commander had the obligation to submit requisitions to adjust supply requirements. Ideally, this dialogue informed automatic shipment data, which was to anticipate and push supplies to the theatre commander and while doing so, the port commander was to update the theatre commander on the status of inbound supplies. The theatre commander would, in turn, provide micro-adjustments to supply data to re-inform the next automatic shipment that went out. In practice, however, neither side fully understood or appreciated their role in the relationship. Inefficiencies were rampant and it would be many months before the system ran in a fashion similar to how it was designed. One estimate suggested that supply items were shipped two to three times during the Torch build-up and pre-staging in the UK.[4] Even today, evidence is literally being unearthed of American supplies having gone astray in the United Kingdom.[5]

In late July 1942 the Allies agreed to begin planning for Operation Torch. What functionally amounted to just over three months of preparation time, Operation Torch was an exercise in improvisation more than in planning. (One is reminded of Caesar's reliance on foraging when supply lines were incapable of keeping up with his army's movements.) Much of the planned supply and its system of distribution was a cannibalization of the Bolero build-up. Unlike Bolero, however, Torch had the added complexity of supporting an actual invasion. That meant shipments did not contain just supplies, but also troops and equipment. Torch planners would use the existing supply mechanisms to create a system that pushed supplies, via automatic supply, forward through a series of pre-planned slow and fast convoys directly to ports in North Africa in order to support a forward build-up of supplies, forces and equipment. While supply inefficiencies often manifested themselves into useless deliveries, it was less an issue of port capacity and more an issue of unneeded supplies and a lack of capacity to move supplies forward from North African ports to the front-line forces. After about six months, however, automatic shipments were turned off in favour of requisition supply. As it happened, by both design and by chance, a sufficient build-up had been achieved and supply inefficiencies were reduced as the theatre commander could requisition what was needed instead of being forced to absorb what was pushed.[6]

The Individual Soldier's Load

The individual loads carried by the Allied soldiers participating in the North African theatre varied greatly from Australian troops serving with the British Commonwealth troops to that of American troops landing under Operation Torch. This divergence appears consistent with the theme that the logistical planners supporting Torch were engaged in discovery learning about the operational art of warfare. Australian troops going into combat at Bardia, Libya and El Alamein, Egypt, carried loads between 22–32kg (48–70 lbs) whereas American forces had loads as great as 60kg (132lbs).[7] This can be compared to the estimated legionary's load of 40–45kg.

In an effort to provide the individual soldier with weapons, protection and sustainment gear for most eventualities, US planners heaped a herculean burden upon its soldiers. The American soldier disembarked from combat shipping with his combat load, individual pack and two barracks bags. The combat load consisted of a personal weapon (officers and non-commissioned officers were issued submachine guns in lieu of pistols), loaded cartridge belt and grenades; protective equipment in the form of helmet, gas mask and life belt; and canteens and emergency rations were included as individual sustainment gear. Between the individual pack and barracks bags, soldiers had to fit the following: three pairs of boots; cotton, woollen and anti-gas uniforms; socks, shirts and undergarments; a raincoat; mosquito repellent, head nets and gloves; desert goggles, dust respirators and neck cloths; two bedrolls; mess kit; entrenching tool; and any other personal articles that might have been desired. Officers were also allowed a musette bag, hand baggage and a trunk locker. This says nothing about a variety of organizational equipment and ordinance that might have been issued to a particular front-line unit such as binoculars, mine detectors, 'bazooka' rocket launchers and other crew-served weapons and ammunition. Surely all this equipment was not 'taken into the fight' as much was expected to be brought forward via motorized lift. Nevertheless, just as Marius' Mules did 2,000 years earlier, soldiers found special places to stow their personal burdens while on campaign. Moreover, the detritus of war found itself lovingly tossed on the beach, along the road and throughout the steppe and plains of North Africa.[8]

The need for both food and water complicated the logistic tether that tied both the Axis and Allied armies to the ports. When it came to food and water, all armies were in a theatre near devoid of both, at least to the scale to support the combatants in theatre. While the situation was more acute in the Western Desert, both the Axis and Allies had to import all their food and most of their water from outside the theatre. This meant it was shipped via the United Kingdom or the United States for the Allies, often in the form of canned rations, and for the Axis water and food was shipped via Italy. Even before operations, US planners recognized the scarcity and additional logistical burden of water needs. American troops were, at the individual level, equipped with water-purifying and water-saving equipment.[9]

Fuel: The Modern Fodder
Moving beyond the individual needs of soldiers, the requirement to feed the armoured cavalry with the fodder of the modern era was critical to the success and failure of the multiple thrusts back and forth between the Axis and Allies in both theatres throughout the North African campaign. While Roman commanders were preoccupied with

the constant need to provide fodder, Allied commanders were similarly concerned with having a steady supply of fuel. Belligerents on both sides made use of any available infrastructure to transport petroleum, oil and lubricants (POL) to their motorized and mechanized forces. For the Allies, planning for fuel rightfully started with planning for the invasion at large.

Using the experience of British planners who already had forces in theatre, Operation Torch planners estimated fuel consumption at 5 gallons per day for wheeled vehicles and 50 gallons per day for tracked vehicles.[10] Vehicles were embarked aboard assault shipping not only with their tanks full, but with additional 5-gallon cans. In addition to a supply company landing at D-Day with POL dumps for air and ground forces being established at D+1, a further seven days of supply was combat-loaded on the assault shipping. Follow-up actions included the re-establishment of a gasoline refinery in the port of Oran and dumps were established at various echelons to support the advancing forces. Distribution methods started at the dumps themselves, but also took advantage of rail lines and pipelines, either existing or laid and tanker trucks used road networks. The most prolific method was to use 55-gallon drums, either independently, or to arrange them on 2½-ton trucks to create field-expedient tankers. Further down at the unit level, 5-gallon cans would be employed to deliver POL to the individual vehicles.[11]

Like the armies of antiquity that stocked up prior to initiating campaign seasons, the Allies, on both fronts, deliberately built up forward stores of POL, munitions, food, water and other supplies prior to kicking off offensive operations. Forward bases were used to increase the elasticity of supply tethers and through an echeloned disposition found logistical efficiencies. Still, the transaction cost of feeding the metal beasts of war was ever-present. Not only were supply convoys moving along a barren landscape particularly vulnerable to air interdiction, but the fact that they themselves caused secondary consumption of the precious fuel they carried (just as pack animals ate the very fodder they carried), meant that a significant portion of rolling stock itself was used to feed troops and combat vehicles with food, fuel and ammunition. Estimates suggest that as much as 50–60 per cent of the Axis-imported POL to North Africa was either consumed or destroyed before it ever made it to the front.[12]

Considering the logistical constraints and the fact that everything from food and fuel to ammunition and parts had to be shipped in, was there any ability to 'live off the land?' In terms of food, water, fuel and combat resupply, there was indeed little of it. Martin Van Creveld in *Supplying War: Logistics From Wallenstein to Patton*, stated that 'operating in the desert, neither the British nor their German opponents had the slightest hope of finding anything useful but camel dung and while the former did at least possess a base of some considerable size in Egypt, the latter were entirely dependent on sea-transport even for their most elementary requirements'.[13] If we extend the concept of living off the land to making use of what is endogenously available in theatre then perhaps captured supplies and equipment and making use of local labour could be thought of as living off the land. As the campaign wore on and Rommel, commander of the Afrika Korps, was ever more desperate for logistical relief, he did not pass up the opportunity to take advantage of the spoils of war. Additionally, there was some limited host-nation support available, but this, like the terrain, exacted a transaction cost when utilizing it.

Moreover, both the Axis and Allies made use of local labour to support port operations and onward logistical movement of supplies to forward staging points. The main host nation support received by the Axis was in the form of port labour in Tripoli. This labour, however, was highly susceptible to being driven off by Allied air raids. The Allies faired a bit better as local labour not only worked the ports unloading everything from consumables to equipment, but made use of indigenous means in the form of local trucks and horse-drawn wagons to transport supplies from the beach to onward staging points. Interestingly, payment was taken in cigarettes, cloth and rations. In Morocco, local labour was employed in railway operations, though they were always under supervision. Allied commanders had a pessimistic view of the quality of local labour on account that it was not only erratic in quantity and quality, but it, too, was highly susceptible to being dissuaded by Axis bombings.

The net effect of the logistical challenges on both sides manifested itself in the North Africa campaign being a battle of ports. Axis and Allied operational strategies alike centred on securing logistics to affect operation jousting. Operationally this meant vying for control of ports and tactically it meant amassing enough supplies forward to support an offensive thrust.

During the early jousting for control of the Western Desert, the Allies took control of Tobruk in Libya in January 1940. The port would be contested a little over a year later in 10 April 1941 during the Axis riposte of Operation Sonnenblume. Unable to defeat the Commonwealth garrison, Rommel initially bypassed and then laid siege to the port of Tobruk. Allied relief and resupply efforts were kept up and the siege was eventually lifted on 27 November 1941. This relief was to last just more than a half of a year when Rommel defeated the British Eighth Army during the Battle of Gazala and maintained enough momentum to seize Tobruk on 21 June 1942. In doing so, the Axis captured a cornucopia of supplies that included 2.5 million gallons of desperately-needed fuel and 2,000 vehicles.[14]

The Western Desert campaign that roared across Libya and Egypt between the Commonwealth nations and first the Italians, later the Italians and Germans, is replete which examples of how logistics influenced operational strategies to either attack of defend on both sides. The fighting of late summer and autumn of 1942 are particularly telling. What would be the final German offensive began on 31 August 1942. Rommel attempted to finish off the British Eighth Army under Montgomery which was located in the vicinity of El Alamein. The subsequent battles of Ruweisat Ridge and Alam el Halfa stopped the Axis advance as the attack culminated in early September. German forces were critically short of ammunition, fuel and reinforcements. The stage was now set for the famed engagement at El Alamein. Montgomery set up a three phase plan: the 'Break-In', seizing positions and key terrain; 'the Dogfight', to wear down German forces and supplies; and 'the Breakout', to defeat the German defensive positions. Over the course of almost two months preceding the engagement, both sides sought to amass supplies and forces. Montgomery, benefiting from both shorter supply lines (given that Rommel was at the end of his tether) and a more robust supply network, won. Montgomery initiated his plan on 23 October and by 3 November, Rommel was desperately short of supplies necessary to sustain the defence. He requested, and received the next day, permission to withdraw.[15]

General Georg Stumme, who was in command of the German forces in the initial days of El Alamein, 'had forbidden the bombardment of British assembly positions on the first night of the attack at El Alamein on account of the Axis' ammunition shortage'.[16] The British Eighth Army, in contrast, amassed an abundance of ammunition. Quoting Liddell Hart, 'The tactics which the British were using follows from their apparent inexhaustible stocks of ammunition. The enormous quantities of ammunition, which the tanks used – sometimes they fired over 30 rounds at one target – were constantly replenished by armoured ammunition carrier.'[17] The disparity, and its resultant consequences, were obvious.

In the final analysis, the contest for North Africa was a battle of logistical attrition. The Allies were able to bring in more troops and their requisite logistical needs than the Axis. In spite of Rommel's tactical genius, Axis troops could not effectively press the attack or prepare for the defence without POL, ammunition and replacement parts and equipment. Once Operation Torch gathered momentum, both the Allied Task Forces coming from the west and the British Eighth Army moving from the east were able to simply out-supply the Axis's Afrika Korps. In doing so, a cadre of Allied operational planners took untested concepts and systems and refined them into something that could effectively sustain armies abroad in an inhospitable region against a determined enemy. The lessons learned by the Allies and paid for in waste, were not to be forgotten.

Allied commanders seemed to have been writing a new playbook. In many ways, Julius Caesar did as well, despite the long history of Roman commanders feeding their armies positioned far from home. Caesar's originality – a greater dependence on requisitioning from allies and former foes and a faith in being able to live off the land – was required due to his aggressiveness. The Allies in the Second World War could not afford such aggressiveness, knowing that the more significant campaign lay in Europe in the future.

Langoustines with Herb Sauce served with Roman Mice

Langoustines (*Nephrops norvegicus*) are small edible lobsters with long, slender claws, native to the north-eastern Atlantic Ocean, the North Sea and the northern Adriatic Sea. They are also called Dublin Bay prawns and Norway lobsters. They typically range in size from 7–10 inches (18–25 cm) from claw to tail. Approximately 30,000 tonnes of langoustine are caught in the United Kingdom waters annually. In the United States, many recipes substitute freshwater crawfish for langoustine, but they are not the same thing.

Ingredients:
8 Langoustines (fresh or frozen)
50ml / ¼ cup olive oil

Spice mix:
¼ tsp cracked black pepper
½ tsp cumin seed
½ tsp coriander seed
⅛ tsp salt

Herb Sauce:
1 cup packed flat parsley leaves
20g / ½ cup chives
75g / ¾ cup packed lovage or celery leaves
3–4 Tbsp olive oil
1–2 Tbsp honey
3 Tbsp red wine vinegar
Salt and pepper to taste

Directions:
In a mortar and pestle, crush the black pepper, cumin and coriander until coarse. Add salt and mix together. Set aside.

Heat a griddle or skillet over medium heat.

Lay langoustines on a cutting board, legs up and with a large knife, cut down the length of them, but not all the way through, splitting to open and expose the meat.

Sprinkle the meat with olive oil and the spice mix.

Place the langoustines, flesh side down, onto the hot griddle or skillet. Let the shellfish roast while you make the sauce.

Place the parsley, chive, lovage or celery leaves on the cutting board and roughly chop together with a large sharp chef's knife.

Place in a medium bowl, add the honey, vinegar and olive oil, mixing together to form a very loose rustic herb sauce.

Remove the langoustines from the pan to a plate or platter, seared flesh side up.

Top with the herb sauce. Serve with Roman Mice.

Serves 4.

Roman Mice
Ingredients:
6 pickled eggs (recipe below)
24 pink peppercorns
24 almonds, shells removed
12 chives

Directions:
Cut eggs in half lengthwise. Place egg halves in a plate flat side down. Insert almonds to make the ears, peppercorns to make the eyes and a chive to make the tail.

Makes 12 mice.

Pickled Eggs
Ingredients:
6 hard-boiled eggs
400ml/2 cups of malt vinegar
5 black peppercorns
5 whole cloves

Directions:
Peel the hard-boiled eggs.

Place vinegar and spices in a saucepan and heat until boiling. Reduce heat and simmer for 10 minutes. Remove pan from heat. Allow eggs and vinegar mixture to cool to room temperature. Place eggs in a clean glass jar. Remove peppercorns and cloves from vinegar mixture. Pour vinegar over the eggs to the top of the container making sure all eggs are completely submerged. Seal jar tightly.

Refrigerate for at least 2 weeks before serving.

Chapter 8

Traces Today

*I follow the same policy toward the enemy as did many doctors
when dealing with physical ailments, namely, that of
conquering the foe by hunger rather than by steel.*

Julius Caesar, quoted by Sextus Julius Frontinus

Julius Caesar's feat of feeding an army so far from home was
unparalleled until well into the next millennium. Even the Crusaders,
beginning in 1096, followed well-established pilgrim routes and could
draw from a developed economy in the Holy Land. Belligerents in the
Thirty Years War (1618–48) relied on plunder and had to keep moving
once they exhausted local resources. Perhaps the next most comparable
military engagement was the American Revolutionary War (1775–83),
when the British had an army of up to 65,000 men operating thousands
of miles from its supply base.[1]

Caesar's supply system balanced supply lines from home bases
with requisition and the exploitation of local sources, whether through
forage, pillage and plunder, or purchasing from local merchants. From
these sources, Caesar's legions were able to supplement their grain,
which they primary got from supply bases, with meat, dairy, beans
and even sauces. While the regular diet of Roman soldiers included a
daily 1kg ration of grain and a little salt, this was regularly flavoured
with oil or some form of fat found locally. Additional ingredients
could sometimes be had from markets and travelling salesmen who
followed the army and set up shop near the soldiers' camps. Without
question, the diet was tedious, but legionaries put up with the tedium
provided the food was plentiful.

With a few noteworthy exceptions, Julius Caesar ensured his troops
had enough food. His great success was a product of his masterful
logistical abilities, which were based on his understanding of the

126

necessity of feeding an army at the end of a stretched supply line. The default situation called for his army combining foodstuffs they had carried with them from Roman sources of supply with local ingredients. This combination is where we can see the influences of Julius Caesar on food history and where culinary traces of his legacy can be detected today.

While there was a distinct Roman military diet, it was never static. Local ingredients influenced the diet in unexpected ways. Moreover, Caesar's armies introduced Roman foods everywhere they went and the pollination had a tremendous influence on the eating habits of the indigenous peoples with whom the Roman military came into contact. Roman supply lines brought wine, oil, grains, even relish, many of which had never been tasted by the local populations. Certain foods made on site, such as cheese, also made their way into indigenous diets.

The geospatial range of Caesar's campaigns brought his legions into contact with different styles of cuisine and what we would now call 'ethnic cooking'. The Roman army sampled and incorporated all of these new foods and the manner in which the indigenous people prepared, cooked and served them, into their own dietary regime. Upon his return to Rome, Caesar, his officers, cooks and legionaries transplanted these ingredients and their culinary styles of preparation back to what was then the capital of the known world, from where the culinary novelties spread the length and breadth of the empire. Their legacy is present today in the ubiquitous European cuisine available nearly everywhere on our planet.

What is fascinating about this process of cross-pollination is the increased dynamism of cuisine, whether Roman, European, African, or Middle Eastern. Soils in one climate rejected seeds that thrived in another climate. Substitutions were made, culinary delights emerged. While discussing archaeological finds dating to the first century AD, R.W. Davies describes how two garrison sites, Caerleon in Britain and Neuss in Germany, had non-indigenous weeds and plants.[2] This indicates that the Romans deliberately introduced rice, chickpeas, olives and figs to Germany so that they might be grown locally to supply the garrison. At the very least, the weeds were intermixed with grain shipments that originated elsewhere (outside of Britain), but were shipped across the Channel to support the legions garrisoned in Britain. The new grains continued to grow and were harvested long after the Romans left northern and central Europe.

Without question, the foods that the Roman army introduced to Britain after Caesar opened the door to that island were more significant.

Numerous vegetables were brought with Roman legions, including onions, garlic, cabbages, peas, celery, turnips, radishes, asparagus and leeks.[3] The Roman army also introduced walnuts, chestnuts, apples, mulberries, cherries, grapes, bay leaves, rosemary, thyme, basil and mint. Cattle, moreover, were shipped to the island, as were chickens and domesticated rabbits. New grains and bread, finally, became an increasingly important staple of the British diet.

The Roman army stationed in the Rhineland during the first and second centuries appears to be the principle conduit for the introduction of foods to Britain. Legions and auxiliary units were regularly transferred to and from this region. Thus, it was not so much a Roman diet that was introduced to Britain (and elsewhere) but a Roman *military* diet. Subsequently, the local populations imitated this military diet.[4]

Cheese also developed due to Julius Caesar and the Roman army. The Gauls introduced the Romans to goat's milk cheese, which was transported to Rome and 'improved', through smoking, in order to eliminate what Romans considered to be a medicinal Gallic flavour. Moreover, the Roman occupation of Gaul introduced new cheeses to northern Europe and spurred the trade of others throughout the region. Caesar himself was said to be partial to an especially pungent cheese from Saint Affrique in the Midi-Pyrénées. The Romans, moreover, brought the first cheese presses to Britain, several of which have been excavated in various archaeological digs at Roman camps.

Caesar's Influence on Viticulture

Perhaps most interesting is Julius Caesar's influence on viticulture. The predominance of *posca* as part of the legionaries' diet should not imply that vintage wines were not available, nor that Caesar had no influence on the development of new wines in Europe or the importation of existing wines into the heart of the Empire. A brief tour of the wine landscape during the period of ancient Rome reveals the extent to which viticulture had developed by Caesar's time – as well as the extent to which his Gallic War and the subsequent incorporation of western Europe into the Roman fold promoted the development of wine and the wine trade.

Grapevines had grown on the Italian peninsula for millennia, though it is unclear exactly when winemaking began there. The Greeks influenced winemaking on the peninsula as early as 800 BC, calling southern Italy Oenotria ('land of vines') because of its ideal location for growing grapevines. The Greeks living there developed vineyards for both local consumption and for trade. Further to the north, near modern Tuscany, the Etruscans had a significant culture of winemaking in the centuries prior to the Roman Republic. Both the Greeks and the Etruscans valued wine not only for consumption but also as a profitable trading commodity.

The regions incorporated into the Roman Republic (and later Empire) had a significant influence on Roman viticulture. Southern Italy, the location of the Greek settlements, came under Roman control by 270 BC. Meanwhile, the Etruscans, who traded with the Gauls, were also incorporated into the Republic. Carthage, moreover, had a significant influence on Roman winemaking, especially after the Punic Wars (264–146 BC). The Carthaginians, in fact, had proven to be particularly sophisticated producers of wine. Mago, a Carthaginian agriculturalist, had written extensively on vine growing. When the Romans captured and destroyed Carthage during the Third Punic War, the libraries were razed. One of the few works that escaped destruction was Mago's agricultural manual, which included books on planting and pruning vines. So valued were Mago's writings that Pliny, Columella, Varro and Gargilius Martialis all subsequently quoted from them.

The golden age of Roman winemaking began during the second century BC, when Roman wines surpassed in reputation – and price – those of the Greeks and continued into the Roman Empire. Pliny the Elder wrote about the tremendous variety of Roman wines in the first century. These included Falernian, the most renowned wine produced in the Empire, grown in vineyards near Rome in Latium. Unfortunately, this vine has disappeared. Alban, which Pliny described as 'extremely sweet and occasionally dry', was the preferred wine of the Roman upper class.[5] It grew in vineyards located at the current site of the Pope's summer residence, Castelgandolfo. Caecuban, considered to be smoother than Falernian and fuller than Alban, was strong and intoxicating. The vineyards that produced this wine were located on the Latium coast. This vine, too, has unfortunately died out.

The golden age produced numerous other locally-grown quality wines. These included Rhaeticum, Hadrianum, Praetutium, Marche and Lunense, among many others. Together, massive quantities of wine were produced and consumed. Historians estimate that Rome consumed over 180 million litres of wine each year, enough for each man, woman and child to drink a bottle per day.[6]

The Roman influence on Gallic wines came via the Iberian Peninsula, which Rome colonized in earnest following the Punic Wars. The Roman development of the colonies included an extensive laying of roads, which made wine a tradable and thus valuable commodity. A look at the areas developed by the Romans – Catalonia, Rioja, Ribera del Duero, Galacia and Hispania Baetica, the main winegrowing areas of Spain today – betray their influence.

Wine from the Iberian Peninsula was exported to Gaul and amphorae, the ceramic vessels used to store wine, have been discovered in Bordeaux, before wine was produced in that region. (In fact, more Iberian wines than Italian wines were traded throughout Europe.) Amphorae from Iberia were found in Aquitaine, Brittany, the Loire Valley, Normandy, Britain and into the Germanic lands. Without the trade and the roads developed by the Romans, the wines of these regions would taste much different today.

As for viticulture in Gaul, while there is evidence that the Greeks had cultivated grape vines near Massalia (Marseilles) several centuries before the Romans arrived, they only planted grape vines in the southern Mediterranean climate, where they also planted olives and figs. The Romans, when they colonized Massalia in 125 BC, developed the region further inland and westward. The Romans, with a more sophisticated understanding of agriculture, understood the benefits of southern-facing hillsides running down to rivers. Narbonne, today the centre of the Languedoc wine region, was founded in 118 BC. Located along the Via Domitia, the first Roman road in Gaul, the Romans promoted trade with the Gallic traders, who paid high prices for Roman wines imported from Spain and Italy.

Amphorae stamped with the seal of Pompeian merchants have been discovered throughout the Roman Empire, including in Bordeaux, Narbonne, Toulouse and Spain. Pompeii was perhaps the most significant centre for wine in the Roman Empire. The Pompeians enthusiastically worshipped Bacchus, the god of wine, and the residents drank copiously. Not only was there significant acreage dedicated to growing vines, but it was also a significant trading centre, with goods going to Rome's outlying provinces. The volcanic eruption that buried Pompeii in 79 AD wreaked havoc on the Roman wine trade. Vineyards were destroyed and the location was eliminated as one of the most significant trading centres on the Italian peninsula. Wine prices rose everywhere. Shortages caused many to uproot grain fields to develop new vineyards. Prices in those new regions of viticulture soon fell, but the development in turn led to a grain shortage. It took until the end of the first century AD before wine and grain prices stabilized again.

Julius Caesar, a century earlier, had no direct interest in developing the wine trade, unless of course his travels exposed him to wines he would subsequently hope to import to Rome for his personal enjoyment. But his army's success in Gaul led to a greater solidification of the Roman wine trade throughout Europe and the Mediterranean region.

Caesar's position in the landscape of Roman viticulture and winemaking was significant for his ability to use the existing infrastructure to quench the thirst of his armies and to promote the colonization of the areas he conquered. During the Gallic War, Caesar's military campaigns brought him through or near what became some of the finest winemaking regions of Europe. After Caesar, the Romans pushed inland along the Rhône Valley. Already by the first century, French wines attracted attention in Rome. Pliny wrote about Vienne, which produced wines for wealthy Romans in the centre of the empire. Strabo noted that there were no decent wines growing in Bordeaux and that wine was being imported from the Midi-Pyrénées region, specifically from the 'high country' of Gaillic. The wines that the Romans cultivated there are still being produced today. These include Duras, Fer, Ondenc and Len de l'El. Eventually, Bordeaux became proficient in producing wine. Its location made it an ideal spot to export wine to the Atlantic, including up the coast to the Roman soldiers stationed in Britain. As the Romans developed further up the Rhône, they developed the regions that are the homes of France's modern wines: Beaujolais, Mâconnais, Côte Chalonnaise and Côte d'Or.

The development of wine in Germania also occurred after Caesar's time, but in the same fashion. Vines were planted in the Rhineland to satisfy the thirst of Roman soldiers stationed there beginning in the first century. This was far cheaper than importing amphorae from Rome, Spain or Bordeaux. Many of the hillsides of the Rhine and Mosel faced south and were thus conducive to sufficient warmth to grow grapes, despite the northerly location. The Rhine, with access to the North Sea, was also an excellent route of supply to soldiers stationed in Britain. Even the hostile Germanic tribes, for example the Alamanni and the Franks, were eager to drink the wine produced in Roman settlements.

Caesar Salad

How many gourmands have ordered a Caesar salad and wondered if its origin traced back to the Roman general? Is the salad a combination of foods brought on supply lines mixed with local ingredients? Was a primitive mix of romaine lettuce, dried bread and seasoned oils the ancestor of that which can be found on restaurant menus throughout the world today?

The short answer is that Caesar salad has little to do with Julius Caesar beyond the longevity of the name *Caesar*. In fact, the only link between Julius Caesar and Caesar salad is the fact that his military exploits so popularized the name Caesar that it was given to Caesar

Cardini, an Italian immigrant who ran restaurants along the Mexican-Californian border. In 1924, Cardini threw together the remaining ingredients of his depleted kitchen to please some guests. Fearing the creation would be found wanting, he aimed to distract the patrons by tossing the salad tableside with dramatic flair. It proved incredibly popular and it was recreated first along the West Coast in the United States and today it can be found on menus throughout the world.

Far more interesting, however, is determining whether it would have even been possible for Julius Caesar to eat a Caesar salad. Again, the short answer is that it no, would not have been possible, but an investigation into the salad's ingredients sheds light on what type of salad the Roman general, or his legions, might have eaten.

The main ingredient of a Caesar salad is, of course, romaine lettuce. An ancestor of romaine lettuce existed millennia ago, with depictions of it etched into ancient Egyptian reliefs. Romaine's other name, *Cos*, refers to the Greek island of Kos, where it existed long before the Greeks so heavily influenced Roman cuisine. Even the contemporary name of the lettuce, 'romaine', is a variation of 'Roman'. The etymology of the word, however, points to papal gardens in Avignon, where the locals in the fourteenth century began calling cos lettuce 'Roman'. Nonetheless, romaine lettuce did grow along the Eastern Mediterranean during Julius Caesar's time. The sturdy leaf was desired in the regional cuisine because it served as an edible utensil while eating foods like tabbouleh. The Romans knew it was healthy, undoubtedly due to its positive effects on digestion. It is claimed that Caesar Augustus erected a statue honouring the lettuce because he believed it cured him from disease.

So, if romaine lettuce existed during Caesar's time, what about a Caesar salad's other ingredients? One can assume that croutons – essentially seasoned bread – would not be difficult to obtain. Today, croutons are made by re-baking or sautéing bread, but it is essentially dried bread. If anything, finding bread that was not dry would have been more of a challenge. Besides, in the event of a salad emergency, they could have always broken up a piece of hard tack.

And what of the dressing? Many of the dressing's ingredients would have been easy to obtain: olive oil, garlic, egg yolks, salt and pepper and wine vinegar. The remaining ingredients – lemon juice, Worcestershire Sauce and Parmesan cheese – would have been more problematic. It is believed that lemons entered Europe from Asia no later than the first century, but they were not widely cultivated. Still, perhaps additional wine vinegar would add a sufficiently sour taste. Perhaps lemon juice was not necessary.

Recreating the taste of Worcestershire Sauce would have been a challenge. John Wheeley Lea and William Henry Perrins, both chemists, first produced Worcestershire Sauce in 1837 using malt vinegar (from barley), molasses, sugar, salt, anchovies, garlic and various spices. Give a centurion a century with those ingredients and it is still unlikely that they would be able to come up with a comparable sauce. Maybe a Caesar salad can do without the Worcestershire Sauce, but we have to admit the salad is moving away from what we enjoy today. Even if we added extra vinegar wine to compensate for the lemon juice and Caesar's chefs combined various ingredients to come to a close approximation of Worcestershire Sauce, the flavour is deviating from what we know to be that of Caesar salad.

The final element that forces us to conclude that Julius Caesar could never have eaten what we know as a Caesar salad is the fact that Parmigiano-Reggiano was not first produced until the Middle Ages and no self-respecting Caesar salad excludes Parmesan cheese, the taste and aroma of which are incomparable.

Coq au Vin

Legend traces coq au vin to Julius Caesar and Gaul. The base of the legend is the French ability to turn rustic foods into culinary genius. However, it was not the Gauls, but the Romans who performed the magic. (Regardless, it was the mixing of Gallic and Roman foods that have led to the pre-eminence of French cuisine.) The legend asserts that certain Gauls gave Julius Caesar a tough old rooster as mocking tribute after he conquered them. Caesar gave it to his cook, who turned it into a delicious meal and gave it back to the Gauls to show Roman superiority.

Is the legend accurate or is it as apocryphal as Caesar's connection to Caesar salad? Again, we can use the same investigative approach, determining whether it was possible to Caesar to have assembled the ingredients into the dish known and loved throughout France.

Unfortunately, there are no primary sources pointing to the veracity of the story. In fact, the first documented evidence of a chicken in wine recipe does not appear until the twentieth century. However, elements of the legend ring true. Conquered peoples did pay tribute after being conquered and this tribute was often in the form of food, both for the soldiers and the commanders. Moreover, Caesar consistently attempted to woo foe and ally alike and inviting them to dinner would have been consistent with this policy. And Caesar certainly had his own cook throughout his time in Gaul and the main ingredients of coq au vin – wine, chicken, mushrooms, lardoons (salted pork fat), salt, pepper, thyme, bay leaf – were readily available, including the vintage red wine, which officers drank rather than *posca*.

It should be kept in mind that there are regional differences in how coq au vin is prepared throughout France and there is no single recipe. The ability to turn basic ingredients into gourmet dishes is the pride of France. The best we can say is that the legend may or may not be true, though it is definitely possible and was consistent with Caesar's modus operandi in Gaul.

Endnotes

Abbreviations:
BGal De Bello Gallico (*The Gallic War*)
BCiv De Bello Civili (*Civil Wars*)
BAfr De Bello Africo (*The African War*)
BAl De Bello Alexandrino (*The Alexandrian War*)

Introduction

1. Julius Caesar, *The Gallic War* (hereafter *BGal*), H.J. Edwards, trans. (Cambridge, MA, 1917), I.23, 39, II.2, VII.3, 10; *Civil Wars* (hereafter *BCiv*), A.G. Prescott, trans. (Cambridge, MA, 1914), 1.16, 54, 2.22, 3.9.
2. Paul Erdkamp, *Hunger and the Sword: Warfare and Food Supply in the Republican Wars (264–30 BC)* (Leiden, 1998), 6.
3. *BGal* I 16,3.
4. *BGal* I 16.
5. *BGal* I 23.

Chapter 1: Julius Caesar, His Wars and The Caesarian Army

1. *BGal* IV 37,1.
2. In the Civil War, Caesar reported that 3,000 riders were sent to Spain, so the number of cavalry seems to have remained relatively stable. *BCiv* 1,39,2.
3. Julius Caesar, *Alexandrian War, African War, Spanish War* (hereafter *BAl, BAfr*), A.G. Way, trans. (Cambridge, MA, 1955), 54, 1–4.
4. Anton Labisch, *Frumentum Commeatusque: Die Nahrungsmittelversorgung der Heere Caesars* (Meisenheim an Glan, 1975), 42–3.

Chapter 2: Food for Battle

1. *BCiv* 1,52.
2. *BCiv* 3,47–48.
3. Hugo Merguet, *Lexikon zu den Schriften Caesars und seiner Fortsetzer* (Hildesheim, 1963).
4. Pliny, *Natural History*, 10 vols. H. Rackham, W.H.S. Jones and D.E. Eichholz, trans. (Cambridge, MA, 1938–62), XVIII 12.
5. Cato, *On Agriculture*, W.D. Hooper and H.B. Ash, trans. (Cambridge, MA: Harvard, 1934), 56.

6. Seneca, *Epistles*, 3 vols. Richard M. Gummere, trans. (Cambridge, MA, 1917–25), 80,7. Cf. Labisch, 33.
7. Labisch, 33.
8. Dio Cassius, *Roman History*, I–IX. Ernest Cary, trans. (Cambridge, MA, 1914–27), 41,28,1.
9. Other uses of '*ciberia*' in *BGal* are to be found at I 5,3; III 18,6; VI 10,2.
10. *BGal* I 15,5; 23,1.
11. *BGal* VII 74,2.
12. *BGal* VII 32,1; 1,16,1.
13. *BGal* I 39,1.
14. Labisch, 35.
15. Herodian, *History of the Empire*, 2 vols. C.R. Whittaker, trans. (Cambridge, MA, 1969–70), 4.7.5.
16. *BGal* VII 17.
17. Ibid.
18. *BGal* VII 55–56.
19. *BGal* V 21,6.
20. *BGal* VI 3,2. See also VI 6,1.
21. *BCiv* 1,48,6. Cf. Labisch, 38–9.
22. *BGal* VI 43,1.
23. *BCiv* 1, 41–46.
24. *Historia Augusta* Hadrian 10.2.
25. *BGal* V.14. Cf. VI.22.
26. Cf. Erdkamp, *Hunger and the Sword*, 33.
27. *BCiv* 2,37,5.
28. *BCiv* 3,47,6.
29. *BGal* IV 1,8. See also Caesar's description of the Germans in VI 22,1: 'For agriculture they have no zeal and the greater part of their food consists of milk, cheese and flesh.'
30. *BGal* V 14,2.
31. *BGal* IV 10,5.
32. *BCiv* 3,48,1.
33. *Historia Augusta* Hadrian 10.2.
34. For example, see *BCiv* 3,58,4.
35. *BCiv* 3,47,6. There are no references to barley in *BGal*.
36. *BCiv* 3.47.
37. Polybius, *The Histories*, 6 vols. W.R. Paton, trans. (Cambridge, MA, 2010–12), VI 38,3.
38. Erdkamp, *Hunger and the Sword*, 35.
39. Jonathan P. Roth, *The Logistics of the Roman Army at War (264 BC – AD 235)* (Leiden, 1998), 248.
40. Richard A. Gabriel, *Soldiers' Lives through History – The Ancient World* (Greenwood Press, 2006).
41. Appian, *Roman History*, I–IV. Horace White, trans. (Cambridge, MA, 1912–13), 2.11; cf. Roth, *Logistics of the Roman Army at War*, 37.

42. Plutarch, *Lives, vol. VIII: Sertorius and Eumenes*. Bernadotte Perrin, trans. (Cambridge, MA, 1919), 3.4.
43. Tacitus, *Histories*, vols. I–III. Clifford H. Moore, trans. (Cambridge, MA, 1925), 1.70.
44. Edward E. Curtis, *The British Army in the American Revolution* (New Haven: Yale University Press, 1926); Dennis E. Showalter, *Soldiers' Lives through History* (Westport, CT: Greenwood Press, 2007), 36–7; Roth, *Logistics of the Roman Army at War*.
45. Appian, *Roman History*, I–IV. Horace White, trans. (Cambridge, MA, 1912–13), 7.40.
46. Rod Phillips, *A Short History of Wine* (New York, 2000), 57–63.
47. Rolf E. Hellex, *Bier im Wort: Ein ergötzliches Zitaten-Kolleg rund um den Gerstensaft aus vier Jahrtausenden* (Nuremberg, 1981), 23–4.
48. Ibid., 24.
49. http://www.bbc.co.uk/history/ancient/romans/vindolanda_01.shtml#three.
50. For a searchable database of the hundreds of Vindolanda Tablets discovered to date, see http://vindolanda.csad.ox.ac.uk.
51. *BGal* IV 11,4.
52. Plutarch, *Lives, vol. V: Aegisilaus and Pompey*. Bernadotte Perrin, trans. (Cambridge, MA, 1917), 72.4; cf. Caesar *BCiv* 3.96.
53. Appian, *BCiv* 2.11.
54. Roth, *Logistics of the Roman Army at War*, 46.
55. Ibid., 57.

Chapter 3: The Invention of Logistics

1. Polybius, 3.89.
2. Quoted in Dio Cassius, 42.49.
3. Roth, *Logistics of the Roman Army at War*, 242.
4. Erdkamp, *Hunger and the Sword*, 96.
5. Livy 31.11,4ff.; 31.19,2ff.; 32.27,2.
6. Livy, 43.6,11ff.
7. Cf. Erdkamp, *Hunger and the Sword*, 98.
8. *BAfr* 20,4; 24,3.
9. Labisch, 87.
10. *BGal* I 16.
11. http://www.military-quotes.com/forum/logistics-quotes-t511.html or http://www.macroknow.com/books/quotes/q-jomini.htm.
12. Joel P. Gleason, *Roman Roads in Gaul: How Communication and Basing Support Operational Reach*. School of Advanced Military Studies (Fort Leavenworth, 2013), 1.
13. Ibid., 29.
14. John Keegan, *Intelligence in War: Knowledge of the Enemy from Napoleon to Al-Qaeda* (London, 2003), 8.

15. Ibid.
16. Roth, *Logistics of the Roman Army at War*, 214–19; William Smith, William Wayte and G.E. Marindin, *A Dictionary of Greek and Roman Antiquities* (London: J. Murray, 1890), 946–54.
17. Elena Taraskina, 'River of Memory', *Minerva* Vol. 21/No. 3 (2010): 28–31.
18. Roth, *Logistics of the Roman Army at War*, 214–19.
19. Ibid.; Keegan, 10.
20. Smith, Wayte and Marindin, 946–54; 'Roman Roads' The Columbia Electronic Encyclopedia, 6th ed. Copyright © 2007, Columbia University http://www.infoplease.com/ce6/history/A0842316.html.
21. N.J.E. Austin and N.B. Rankov, *Exploratio: Military and political intelligence in the Roman world from the Second Punic War to the Battle of Adrianople* (London, 1995), 113.
22. Ibid., 114–15.
23. Ibid., 112–13.
24. Ibid., 115–18.
25. *BGal* VI 36,3.
26. *BGal* VII 20,9.
27. *BGal* II 24,2.
28. *BCiv* 1.52.4.
29. *BAl* 73,3.
30. Cf. Labisch, 100–1.
31. Labisch, 106.
32. Ibid.
33. *BGal* IV 13,4; IV 22,3.
34. *BGal* V 24,3. The Marcus Crassus cited here should not be confused with Marcus Licinius Crassus, the member of the First Triumvirate with Caesar and Pompey.
35. *BGal* V 46,1.
36. *BGal* VI 47,2.
37. *BGal* VI 6,1.
38. *BGal* VII 81.
39. *BGal* VIII 2.
40. *BCiv* 3,62,4.
41. *BAl* 25,3.
42. Cf. Labisch, 111–12.
43. *BGal* V 8,1.
44. Labisch, 112–13.
45. *BGal* VII 3,1.
46. Cf. Labisch, 116.
47. *BGal* VII 10,4.
48. *BGal* VII 57,1.

Chapter 4: Supply Lines – Definitions and Practicalities

1. Vegetius, *Epit.* 3.26.
2. See Labisch.

3. Lawrence Keppie, *The Making of the Roman Army: From Republic to Empire* (London, 1984), 66–7.
4. John Peddie, *The Roman War Machine* (Stroud, 2004), 50–5; Roth, *Logistics of the Roman Army at War*, 68–77; Vegetius, 19–23; Russ Cowan, *Roman Legionary: 58 BC–AD 69* (Oxford, 2003), 25–45.
5. Cowan, *Roman Legionary*, 25–45; Roth, *Logistics of the Roman Army at War*, 77–91; Vegetius, 23–5, 38–9 and 56–7.
6. Roth, *Logistics of the Roman Army at War*, 169–89.; Peddie, 42–7 and 59–79; Vegetius, 23–5, 38–9 and 56–7.
7. Cf. Erdkamp, *Hunger and the Sword*, 23, 47.
8. Cf. Roth, *Logistics of the Roman Army at War*, 191; Erdkamp, *Hunger and the Sword*, 53.
9. Roth, *Logistics of the Roman Army at War*, 191.
10. *BAfr* 24. Cf. Erdkamp, *Hunger and the Sword*, 54.
11. On conditions of Roman granaries, see Marcus Junkelmann, *Die Legionen des Augustus. Der römische Soldat im archäologischen Experiment* (Mainz, 1986).
12. *BAfr* 21.
13. Erdkamp, *Hunger and the Sword*, 58.
14. *BGal* IV 20.4.
15. *BGal* III 9.6.
16. Roth, *Logistics of the Roman Army at War*, 197.
17. *BCiv* 1.48.
18. Cf. Erdkamp, *Hunger and the Sword*, 74.
19. *BGal* I 38.
20. *BAfr* 36. Cf. Roth, *Logistics of the Roman Army at War*, 171.
21. *BGal* VII 10.
22. *BAfr*, 47.
23. *BGal* 6.44.
24. Labisch, 88.
25. *BGal* II 5,5; 9,5.
26. *BGal* V 1,1; 2,2.
27. *BGal* VII 10,1.
28. Ibid.
29. *BGal* VII 11,1.
30. *BGal* VII 34,1.
31. *BGal* VI 5,6.
32. *BGal* VI 32,5.
33. *BGal* III 1.
34. *BGal* III 3.
35. Labisch, 96.
36. *BGal* IV 29,4.
37. *BGal* V 47,2.
38. *BGal* I 54,2; II 35; III 29,3; IV 38,4; VII 90, 4–7; VIII 46, 3–4; VIII 54,4.
39. *BGal* V 24,1; Cf. Labisch, 97.
40. Roth, *Logistics of the Roman Army at War*, 89.

41. *BGal* IV 30.
42. *BAfr* 47.
43. Tacitus, *Ann.* 2.5; Polybius, 3.68.
44. *BGal* I 40.
45. *BGal* I 24,3; II 17,2; III 24,3; VII 18,4; *BAfr.* 9,1; 69,2; 75,3.
46. *BGal*, VI 32,5; VII 10,4.
47. *BAfr*, 47,3.
48. Examples of this include the headquarters in Samarobriva (*BGal* V 47,2) and Noviodunum (*BGal* VII 55, 2.)
49. *BGal* VII 55, 1–3.
50. *BGal* VII 57,1; 62,10.
51. *BCiv* 1,69,2.
52. *BCiv* 3,6,1; *BAfr* 47,3.

Chapter 5: On the March

1. Junkelmann.
2. *BAfr* 74.
3. Appian, *BCiv*, 2.15.
4. Tacitus, Ann. 1.63.
5. *BGal* 2.17.
6. Peddie, 59.
7. Vegetius, *On Roman Military Matters*, 64–7.
8. Ibid; Peddie, 59–79; Cowan, *Roman Legionary*, 44–5 and 62.
9. *BGal* I, 49; Cowan, *Roman Legionary*, 44–5 and 62.
10. Peddie, 72–6.
11. D.A.S. John (ed.), *Julius Caesar: 55 & 54 BC Expeditions to Britain or De Bello Gallico IV, 20–36 & V, 8–2* (London, 1969), 28–31.
12. *BGal* I, 15.
13. *BGal* I, 31–54; Roth, *Logistics of the Roman Army at War*, 279–328.
14. *BGal* IV 32,1; VIII 17.
15. *BAfr* 11.
16. *BAfr* 65.
17. *BCiv* 2.37.
18. *BCiv* 1.81; *BAfr* 5.
19. Appian, *BCiv* 2.7.44.
20. *BCiv* 1.84.
21. *BGal* 5.26.
22. *BAfr* 10.
23. *Historia Augusta Tyr. Trig* 18.6–9.
24. *BGal* VII 14.
25. *BGal* VIII 10,4; 1,4,0,3.
26. *BGal* VII 20,9, VIII 10,4.
27. *BAfr* 24. Cf. Roth, *Logistics of the Roman Army at War*, 65.
28. *BGal* VII 74,2.
29. *BCiv* 3.58.

30. *BGal* VII 16.
31. *BGal* V 17, 2–5; VII 16,3; 20,9; VIII 10,3,4; 16,4; *BCiv* 1,40,3–7; *BAfr* 24,2.
32. *BGal* V 17,2; VIII 11,2; 1,40,3.
33. *BGal* VIII 10,1.
34. *BGal* V 17,2.
35. *BGal* VIII 17,2; *BAfr* 12,1.
36. *BGal* VIII 17,3.
37. Labisch, 67.
38. *BGal* II 2.
39. Julius Caesar, *The Gallic War* (Mineola NY, 2006), 3–16 (Book I, 5–31).
40. Josephus, *BJ* 3.85–6.
41. *BGal* IV 30,1; 31,2.
42. *BGal* VII 56,5.
43. See *BGal* IV 38,3; Cf. Erdkamp, *Hunger and the Sword*, 123–4.
44. *BGal* VII 14; see also VII 64.
45. *BGal* VII 16.
46. *BGal* VII 13.
47. *BGal* VII 32.
48. *BCiv* 3.43.3.
49. *BCiv* 3.85.
50. *BAfr* 65.
51. Vegetius, *On Roman Military Matters*, 56.
52. Paul Erdkamp, 'The Corn Supply of the Roman Armies during the Third and Second Centuries BC', *Zeitschrift fur Alte Geschichte* 44 (1995): 168–91.
53. Julius Caesar, *The Gallic War* (Mineola NY, 2006), 20 (Book I, 40).
54. Erdkamp, 'The Corn Supply of the Roman Armies during the Third and Second Centuries BC', 174.
55. Julius Caesar, *The Gallic War* (Mineola NY, 2006), 80–1 (Book V, 20–22).
56. *BGal* I 16.1.
57. *BGal* I 16.3.
58. *BGal* I 16.2.
59. *BGal* I 23.1.
60. Labisch, 46.
61. *BGal* I 37,5; I 38,3, 39,1.
62. *BGal* I 40,11, 48,2.
63. *BGal* I 39, 6.
64. *BGal* I 40, 11.
65. Labisch, 52.
66. *BGal* II 3,1–3.
67. *BGal* II 5,5; 9,5.
68. Labisch, 53.
69. *BGal* I 16, 1–4.
70. For an example of the use of riverboats, see *BGal* VII, 55,8.
71. *BGal* I 48,2; 49,1.
72. *BGal* II 5,5.

73. *BGal* III 23,7.
74. *BGal* VII, 34,1.
75. *BGal* V 24,1.
76. *BGal* VI 44,3.
77. *BGal* VII 2,1; 4,1; 5,7; 7,1.
78. *BGal* VII 10,4.
79. *BGal* VII 54–55.
80. *BGal* VII 17,3.
81. Quoted in Erdkamp, *Hunger and the Sword*, 14.
82. See examples *BCiv* 1,40,1; 52,4; *BAfr* 26,1.
83. *BCiv* 1,60,30.
84. *BCiv* 1,48,4.
85. *BCiv* 1,51,1.
86. *BCiv* 3,40,4.
87. *BCiv* 3,42,2.
88. *BAfr* 9,1.
89. *BCiv* 1,60,3.5.
90. *BCiv* 3,42,3.4.
91. *BCiv* 3,81,3; 84,1; 85,2.
92. *BGal* II 33,6.
93. *BGal* VIII 44,1.
94. *BCiv* 3,40, 4–7.
95. Tacitus, *Ann* 12.43.
96. Julius Caesar, *The Gallic War* (Mineola NY, 2006), 80 (Book V, 19).
97. Ibid.
98. *BAfr* 3.
99. Roth, *Logistics of the Roman Army at War*, 149.
100. *BAfr* 54.
101. Erdkamp, *Hunger and the Sword*, 13.
102. *BGal* VIII 3,1f.; Erdkamp, *Hunger and the Sword*, 148.
103. Roth, *Logistics of the Roman Army at War*, 96–101
104. Sue Stallibrass and Richard Thomas (eds), *Feeding the Roman Army: The Archaeology of Production and Supply in NW Europe* (Oxford, 2008), 8.
105. *BGal* VI 37,2; *BAfr* 75.
106. R.W. Davies, 'The Roman Military Diet', *Britannia* 2 (1971): 124 and 128.
107. Ibid., 134–5.

Chapter 6: Logistics and Strategy

1. Vegetius, *On Roman Military Matters*, 56.
2. Ibid., 57.
3. Sextus Julius Frontinus, *Strategems. Aqueducts of Rome*. Charles E. Bennett, trans. (Cambridge, MA, 1925), 4.7.1.
4. Roth, *Logistics of the Roman Army at War*, 309.
5. See for example *BGal* I 5,2; 28,3; II 7,2.3; IV 4,2; VII 14,5.
6. *BGal* I 3, 1–2.

7. Cf. Labisch, 125–6.
8. *BGal* III 10,3.
9. *BGal* III 8,3; IV 5.
10. *BGal* I 24,5.
11. *BGal* I 52,4.
12. *BGal* II 19,6–8.
13. *BGal* III 20.
14. *BGal* IV 29–30.
15. *BGal* IV 34, 43.
16. *BGal* I 16; I 23,1.
17. *BGal* I 48,2; 49,1.
18. *BCiv* 3,47.5.
19. *BCiv* 1,38,4.
20. *BCiv* 1,48,5.
21. *BCiv* 1,48,4; 1,40,3.4.
22. *BCiv* 1,48,7; 1,50; 1,51; 1,54,1.
23. *BCiv* 1,52,2.
24. *BCiv* 1,53; 2,17,4.
25. *BCiv* 1,54,5.
26. *BCiv* 1,59,1; 1, 56–58.
27. *BCiv* 1,60,3.5; 1,61,2.
28. *BCiv* 1,61,2–4.
29. *BCiv* 1,68–70.
30. *BCiv* 1,84,3–5.
31. *BCiv* 3,49,1.
32. *BCiv* 3,48,2.
33. Appian, *Roman History*, 2,53.
34. *BCiv* 3,48,1.2.
35. *BAfr.* 24,4.
36. *BCiv* 3.47.
37. *BCiv* 1.73–78.
38. *BGal* I 23; VII 14.
39. *BGal* VII 64. See also VII 14.
40. *BCiv* 3.85.
41. Roth, *Logistics of the Roman Army at War*, 298.
42. *BAl* 25.
43. Tacitus, *Annals*, 2.5
44. Polybius, *Histories*, 3.68.
45. *BGal* VII 16.

Chapter 7: A Modern North African Campaign

1. David T. Zabecki, 'World War II: North Africa Campaign', *World War II Magazine*, March 1997; Jay Hatton, 'Logistics and the Desert Fox', *Army Logistician*, January–February 2001.

2. Mark D. Kitchen, 'The North Africa Campaign: A logistical Assessment'. Master's Thesis, U.S. Army Command and General Staff College, Fort Leavenworth, Kansas, 1991, 19–21, 49, 87–8.
3. Ibid., 19–21, 72; Roland G. Ruppenthal, *United States Army in World War II, The European Theater of Operations, Logistical Support of the Armies* Vol. I (May 1941–September 1944) (District of Columbia, 1995), 90–7; Hatton; Robert W. Coakley and Richard M. Leighton, *United States Army In World War II, The War Department, Global Logistics and Strategy 1940–1943* (District of Columbia, 1995), 466–8, 477–8; Zabecki.
4. Ruppenthal, 97.
5. Ibid., 90–7; BBC News, 'US Army sun cream unearthed on Salisbury Plain' http://www.bbc.com/news/uk-england-wiltshire-33378014, downloaded 1 August 2015.
6. Coakley and Leighton, 456–78.
7. Robert Orr, 'The History of the Soldier's Load', *Australian Army Journal*, vii (2) (2010), 74, 78.
8. Coakley and Leighton, 440–1, 452.
9. Ibid., 440; John D. Caviggia, 'British and German Logistics Support during the World War II North African Campaign'. Individual Study Project, US Army War College (Carlisle Barracks, Pennsylvania, 1990), 7, 9.
10. Kitchen, 82.
11. Ibid., 49, 80–6; Caviggia, 14–15, 24; Coakley and Leighton, 443.
12. Hatton; Caviggia, 31.
13. Hatton.
14. Zabecki; Caviggia, 13; Kitchen, 9.
15. Zabecki; Hatton; Kitchen, 9–11; Caviggia, 26–8.
16. Caviggia, 26.
17. Ibid., 27.

Chapter 8: Traces Today

1. Arthur Bowler, *Logistics and the Failure of the British Army in America, 1775–1783* (Princeton, N.J.: Princeton University Press, 1975), 40.
2. Davies, 133–4.
3. Leeks, in fact, later became so significant in Wales that a leek was included as a national emblem. Legend has it that Saint David, the patron saint of Wales (died 589), ordered his soldiers to wear leeks on their helmets in a battle against the Saxons that took place in a leek field. To this day, the Welsh attach leeks to their clothing on Saint David's Day (March 1) and on days that the national rugby team is playing in international matches.
4. Anthony King, 'Animal Bones and the Dietary Identity of Military and Civilian Groups in Roman Britain, Germany and Gaul', in T.F.C Blagg (ed.), *Military and Civilian in Roman Britain: Cultural Relationships in a Frontier Province* (Oxford: B.A.R., 1984), 187–217.
5. Hugh Johnson, *Vintage: The Story of Wine* (New York, 1989), 62.
6. Phillips, 35–45.

Bibliography

Primary Sources
Julius Caesar
Caesar, Gaius Julius, *The Gallic War*. Translated by H.J. Edwards. Cambridge, MA: Harvard University Press, 1917.
_____, *Civil Wars*. Translated by A.G. Peskett. Cambridge, MA: Harvard University Press, 1914.
_____, *Alexandrian War, African War, Spanish War*. Translated by A.G. Way. Cambridge, MA: Harvard University Press, 1955.
_____, *The Gallic War*. Mineola, NY: Dover Publications, 2006.

Other
Apicius, *Cookery and Dining in Imperial Rome*. Edited and Translated by Joseph Dommers Vehling. London and Toronto: Constable and General Publishing, 1936.
Appian, *Roman History*, I–IV. Translated by Horace White. Cambridge, MA: Harvard University Press, 1912–13.
Cato and Varro, *On Agriculture*. Translated by W.D. Hooper and H.B. Ash. Cambridge, MA: Harvard University Press, 1934.
Dio Cassius, *Roman History*, I–IX. Translated by Ernest Cary. Cambridge, MA: Harvard University Press, 1914–27.
Frontinus, Sextus Julius, *Strategems. Aqueducts of Rome*. Translated by Charles E. Bennett. Cambridge, MA: Harvard University Press, 1925.
Historia Augusta, vol. I. Translated by David Maggie. Cambridge, MA: Harvard University Press, 1921.
Herodian, *History of the Empire*, 2 vols. Translated by C.R. Whittaker. Cambridge, MA: Harvard University Press, 1969–70.
Josephus, *The Jewish War*. Translated by H.St.J. Thackeray. Cambridge, MA: Harvard University Press, 1927.
Livy, *History of Rome*, 14 vols. Translated by B.O. Foster, Frank Gardner Moore and Alfred C. Schlesinger. Cambridge, MA: Harvard University Press, 1919–59.
Pliny, *Natural History*, 10 vols. Translated by H. Rackham, W.H.S. Jones and D.E. Eichholz. Cambridge, MA: Harvard University Press, 1938–62.
Plutarch, *Lives, vol. VIII: Sertorius and Eumenes*. Translated by Bernadotte Perrin. Cambridge, MA: Harvard University Press, 1919.
_____, *Lives, vol. V: Aegisilaus and Pompey*. Translated by Bernadotte Perrin. Cambridge, MA: Harvard University Press, 1917.

Polybius, *The Histories*, 6 vols. Translated by W.R. Paton. Cambridge, MA: Harvard University Press, 2010–12.

Renatus, Flavius Vegetius, *On Roman Military Matters*. Translated from the Latin by Lieutenant John Clarke in 1767. St. Petersburg, FL: Red and Black, 2010.

Seneca, *Epistles*, 3 vols. Translated by Richard M. Gummere. Cambridge, MA: Harvard University Press, 1917–25.

Tacitus, *Agricola. Germania. Dialogue on Oratory*. Translated by M. Hutton and W. Peterson. Cambridge, MA: Harvard University Press, 1914.

_____, *Annals*, 2 vols. Translated by John Jackson. Cambridge, MA: Harvard University Press, 1937.

Secondary Sources

Abdy, R., *Pocket Dictionary of the Roman Army*. London: The British Museum Press, 2008.

Amato, F. M., *La Cucina di Roma Antica*. Rome: Neeton Compton editori, 2007.

Austin, N.J.E. and N.B. Rankov, *Exploratio: Military and Political Intelligence in the Roman World from the Second Punic War to the Battle of Adrianople*. London: Routledge, 1995.

Axelrod, Alan, *Julius Caesar CEO*. New York: Sterling, 2012.

Beard, Mary, *The Fires of Vesuvius*. Cambridge, MA: Belknap Press, 2010.

Beerden, Kim, 'A Conspicuous Meal: Fattening Dormice, Snails and Thrushes in the Roman World', in *Petits Propos Culinaires 90: Essays and Notes on Food, Cookery and Cookery Books*. London: Prospect Books, 2010.

Birley, Robin, *Vindolanda: A Roman Frontier on Hadrian's Wall*. London: Thames & Hudson, 1977.

Boak, Arthur, *A History of Rome to 565 AD*. New York: Macmillan, 1930.

Bowler, Arthur, *Logistics and the Failure of the British Army in America, 1775–1783*. Princeton, N.J.: Princeton University Press, 1975.

Brunt, P.A., 'Pay and Superannuation in the Roman Army'. *Papers of the British School at Rome* 18 (1950): 50–71.

Caviggia, John D., 'British and German Logistics Support during the World War II North African Campaign'. Individual Study Project, U.S. Army War College, Carlisle Barracks, Pennsylvania, 1990.

Coakley, Robert W. and Richard M. Leighton, *United States Army in World War II, The War Department, Global Logistics and Strategy 1940–1943*. District of Columbia: Center Of Military History United States Army, 1995.

Cowan, Russ, *Roman Legionary: 58 BC–AD 69*. Oxford: Osprey Publishing, 2003.

_____, *Roman Guardsman 62 BC–AD 324*. New York: Osprey Publishing, 2014.

Curtis, Edward E., *The British Army in the American Revolution*. New Haven: Yale University Press, 1926.

Dalby, Andrew and Sally Grainger, *The Classical Cookbook*. Los Angeles: The J. Paul Getty Museum, 1996.

D'Amato, Raffaele and Graham Sumner, *Arms and Armour of the Imperial Roman Soldier: From Marius to Commodus, 112 BC–AD 192*. London: Frontline Books, 2009.

Dando-Collins, Steven, *The Great Fire of Rome*. Cambridge: Da Capo Press, 2010.

Davies, R.W., 'The Roman Military Diet'. *Britannia* 2 (1971): 122–142.

Dosi, A. and F. Schnell, *Vita e Costumi dei Romani Antichi* (Vol I.). Rome: Edizioni Quasar, 1986.

_____, *Le abitudini alimentari dei Romani*. Rome: Edizioni Quasar, 1986.

_____, *I Romani in cucina*. Rome: Edizioni Quasar, 1986.

Elliot, Alistair (trans), *Roman Food Poems*. Devon: Prospect Books, 2003.

Erdkamp, Paul, 'The Corn Supply of the Roman Armies during the Third and Second Centuries BC'. *Historia: Zeitschrift für Alte Geschichte* 44, no. 2. (1995): 168–191.

_____, *Hunger and the Sword: Warfare and Food Supply in Roman Republican Wars (264–30 BC)* (Dutch Monographs on Ancient History and Archaeology). Leiden: Brill, 1998.

_____ (ed.), *The Roman Army and the Economy*. Amsterdam: J.C. Gieben, 2002.

Everitt, Anthony, *Augustus*. New York: Random House, 2006.

_____, *Hadrian. The Triumph of Rome*. New York: Random House, 2009.

_____, *The Rise of Rome*. New York: Random House, 2012.

Fields, Nic, *The Roman Army: The Civil Wars 88–31 BC*. New York: Osprey, 2008.

_____, *Warlords of Republican Rome: Caesar versus Pompey*. Casemate: Havertown, 2008.

_____, *Julius Caesar: Leadership, Strategy, Conflict*. Oxford: Osprey, 2010.

_____, *Pompey*. New York: Osprey, 2012.

Freisenbruch, Annelise, *Caesar's Wives*. New York: Free Press, 2010.

Gabriel, Richard A., *Soldiers' Lives through History – The Ancient World*. Westport, CT; Greenwood Press, 2006.

Giacosa, Ilaria Gozzini, *A Taste of Ancient Rome*. Translated from Italian by Anna Herklotz. Chicago: The University of Chicago Press, 1992.

Gleason, Joel P., *Roman Roads in Gaul: How Communication and Basing Support Operational Reach*. School of Advanced Military Studies. Fort Leavenworth: United States Army Command and General Staff College, 2013.

Goldsworthy, Adrian, *Caesar: Life of a Colossus*. New Haven: Yale University Press, 2006.

_____, *Roman Warfare*. London: Phoenix, 2007.

_____, *Augustus: First Emperor of Rome*. New Haven: Yale University Press, 2014.

_____, *Pax Romana: War, Peace and Conquest in the Roman World*. New Haven: Yale University Press, 2017.

Grant, Mark, *Anthimus on the Observance of Foods*. London: Prospect Books, 1996.

Griess, Thomas E., series editor Elmer C. May, Gerald P. Stadler and John F. Votaw, *Ancient and Medieval Warfare*. Wayne, NJ: Avery, 1984.

Griffin, Miriam T., *Nero: The End of a Dynasty*. London: Yale University Press, 1984.

Hatton, Jay, 'Logistics and the Desert Fox'. *Army Logistician*, January–February 2001.

Hellex, Rolf E., *Bier im Wort: Ein ergötzliches Zitaten-Kolleg rund um den Gerstensaft aus vier Jahrtausenden*. Nuremberg: Hans Carl, 1981.

Holland, Richard, *Augustus: Godfather of Europe*. Phoenix Mill: Sutton, 2004.

Hunt, Patrick N., *Hannibal*. New York: Simon & Schuster, 2017.

James, Simon, *Rome & the Sword*. New York: Thames & Hudson, 2011.

John, D.A.S., *Caesar: 55 & 54 B.C Expeditions to Britain*. London: Bristol Classical Press, 2002.

Johnson, Hugh, *Vintage: the Story of Wine*. New York: Simon & Schuster, 1989.

Junkelmann, Marcus, *Die Legionen Des Augustus: Der römische Soldat im archäologischen Experiment*. Mainz am Rhein: Philipp von Zabern, 1986.

_____, *Panis militaris. Die Ernährung des römischen Soldaten oder der Grundstoff der Macht*. Philipp von Zabern: Mainz, 1997.

Kahn, Arthur D., *The Education of Julius Caesar*. New York: Schocken Books, 1986.

Keaveney, Arthur, *Lucullus: A Life*. London: Routledge, 1992.

Keegan, John, *Intelligence in War: Knowledge of the Enemy from Napoleon to Al-Qaeda*. London: Hutchinson, 2003.

_____, *Intelligence in War: The Value – and Limitations – of What the Military Can Learn about the Enemy*. New York: Vintage, 2004.

Keppie, Lawrence, *The Making of the Roman Army: From Republic to Empire*. London: Batsford, 1984.

King, Anthony, 'Animal Bones and the Dietary Identity of Military and Civilian Groups in Roman Britain, Germany and Gaul', in T.F.C. Blagg, *Military and Civilian in Roman Britain: Cultural Relationships in a Frontier Province* (Oxford: B.A.R., 1984), 187–217.

Kitchen, Mark D., 'The North Africa Campaign: A logistical Assessment'. Master's Thesis, U.S. Army Command and General Staff College, Fort Leavenworth, Kansas, 1991.

Kleberg, Tönnes, *In den Wirtshäusern und Weinstuben des antiken Rom*. Berlin: Akademie-Verlag, 1963.

Knapik, Joseph, 'Loads Carried By Soldiers: Historical, Physiological, Biomechanical and Medical Aspects'. Technical Report T19–89, US Army Research Institute of Environmental Medicine: Natick, MA, 1989.

Labisch, Anton, *Frumentum Commeatusque: Die Nahrungsmittelversorgung der Heere Caesars*. Meisenheim an Glan: Hain, 1975.

Merguet, Hugo, *Lexikon zu den Schriften Cäsars und seiner Fortsetzer*. Hildesheim: Olms,1963.

Mierse, William E., *Temples and Towns in Roman Iberia*. Los Angeles: University of California Press, 1999.

Orr, Robert, 'The History of the Soldier's Load'. *Australian Army Journal*, vii (2), 2010: 67–88.

Peddie, John, *The Roman War Machine*. Stroud: Sutton, 2004.

Phillips, Rod, *A Short History of Wine*. New York: HarperCollins, 2000.

Renfrew, Jane, *Roman Cookery: Recipes & History*. London: English Heritage, 2004.

Roth, Jonathan, 'The Size and Organization of the Roman Imperial Legion'. *Historia: Zeitschrift für Alte Geschichte* 43, no. 3. (1994): 346–362.

_____, *The Logistics of the Roman Army at War (264 BC–AD 235)*. Leiden: Brill, 1998.

_____, *Roman Warfare*. Cambridge: Cambridge University Press, 2009.

Ruppenthal, Roland G., *United States Army in World War II, The European Theater of Operations, Logistical Support of the Armies*. Vol. I (May 1941–September 1944). District of Columbia: Center Of Military History United States Army, 1995.

Showalter, Dennis E., *Soldiers' Lives through History*. Westport, CT: Greenwood Press, 2007.

Siebler, Michael, *Roman Art*. Cologne: Taschen, 2007.

Simkins, Michael, *The Roman Army from Caesar to Trajan*. London: Osprey, 1984.

Smith, William, William Wayte and G.E. Marindin, *A Dictionary of Greek and Roman Antiquities*. London: J. Murray, 1890.

Stallibrass, Sue and Richard Thomas (eds), *Feeding the Roman Army: The Archaeology of Production and Supply in NW Europe*. Oxford: Oxbow Books, 2008.

Taraskina, Elena, 'River of Memory'. *Minerva* 21, no. 3. (May/June 2010): 28–31.

Townend, Gavin, *Caesar's War in Alexandria*. Wauconda: Bolchazy-Carducci, 1988.

Zabecki, David T., 'World War II: North Africa Campaign'. *World War II Magazine*, March 1997. Published online June 12, 2006. http://www.historynet.com/world-war-ii-north-africa-campaign.htm [accessed April 12, 2015].

Index